with best regards
Barbara & John

THE SHOOTING AT BRANSCOMBE OLD PITS

A Nineteenth-century Devon Mystery

Barbara Farquharson & John Torrance

Drawings by Cory Lyons

THE BRANSCOMBE PROJECT

This book is dedicated to the people of Branscombe

ISBN No. 978-0-9555644-3-7

Published by the Branscombe Project 2009

www.branscombeproject.org.uk

Printed by Creeds the Printers, Bridport, DT6 5NL

CONTENTS

ILLUSTRATIONS

Plates

between pages 10 and 11, 16 and 17, and 140 and 141

Full Page Figures

Plates 1 - 2, 4 - 6, 8 - 10 courtesy Branscombe Parish Council; plates 3 & 7 courtesy Geoff Squire; plates 11 & 12 courtesy Rae Cload; figures 1 & 4 courtesy Robin Somers; figures within the text courtesy Branscombe Parish Council, Bill Carpenter, Rae Cload, Jane Harris (Holman), Geoff Squire, Sid Sweetland. Drawings by Cory Lyons; maps by the authors.

Even the dead ask only for justice
-- D. H. Lawrence

PREFACE

Place: Branscombe, seaside village
East Devon
Time: Moonlit night, September 1883
Event: John Perryman, elderly man,
much loved, shot dead on
his way home from harvest
Reaction: Consternation, disbelief, anger
Outcome: A hundred and twenty-five
years later & still no-one
knows who did it

Telling the story: the width and depth of it

The victim of the shooting, John Perryman, was a farm worker. The man accused of the murder, William Dean Dowell, had worked his way up from ploughboy to carpenter. They were working-class people in a small rural backwater in East Devon, and for the divisional police superintendent the case seemed to require no great exertion. He assumed that it was the result of a village brawl that had got out of hand and led to the death of an innocent man. His investigation hardly merits the name, and when William Dean Dowell and his two supposed accomplices came before the magistrates at Honiton, they stopped the case for lack of evidence.

There it was left. No one involved was of any importance. There was no reopening of the inquiry, no attempt to find the real culprit. The villagers remained in a state of confusion and mistrust and eventually took matters in their own hands, with distressing results.

But in fact the accused, William Dean Dowell, was not such an ordinary man. He had got an apprenticeship, left the village, worked in Wales, Birmingham and London, saved money, listened to the leading Liberal politicians of the day and become radicalised. When, some time before the shooting, he returned to Branscombe he was almost a stranger, welcomed by some, mistrusted by others.

When it was all over, he dashed off a pamphlet, *The Branscombe Murder, The Life of William Dean Dowell, the Accused Murderer*. It was published by his trade union and cost 3d. It is a marvellous document – immoderate, desperate, and, to a degree, self-serving. At one level it was simply an attempt to clear his name. He offered a detailed alibi and tried to persuade the person responsible for shooting John Perryman to come forward. At another level, rather more self-consciously and perhaps encouraged by his trade union publishers, he penned a sweeping indictment of late nineteenth-century rural poverty, landlordism and social inequality. The rural working class had just been given the vote, and he used his pamphlet as a rallying cry for the Liberal cause.

Without Dowell's pamphlet we would probably not have started this book. But with it, and with all the other sources available to explore a tiny local story in its wider political and social setting, it was irresistible.

What sort of book is this? It is not fiction; not 'faction'. We are not putting words into people's mouths, or thoughts into their heads. Our account is based on facts — nuggets of information gleaned from many different sources. But, of course, facts are never neutral — they are always selected, preserved and coloured by the historical moment. And we too bring our own ideas about the making of social landscapes to our interpretation. Inevitably, we make our own judgments. Some readers will no doubt think we are too soft on Bill Dowell, and we agree that we like his being a bit of an odd-ball, an outsider, and a stirrer-up of village opinion. We have taken as our motto a remark by D.H. Lawrence: 'Even the dead ask only for justice'. Lawrence added 'not for praise or exoneration' [1] but in Bill Dowell's case we think justice demands exoneration, for his reputation never recovered.

This is the story of a killing, a sudden dramatic event that broke the quiet, though often desperate, round of village life. Suicide was not all that uncommon in Branscombe, but murder was virtually unknown. But was John Perryman murdered, or could his death have been simply an accident? We have used the historical sources to tell the story of the shooting, the hearings, and the aftermath. We have also used clues from oral history, and have 'footstepped' the rough terrain where the shooting occurred. [2] We think – hope – that we have come a little closer to explaining what happened on that fateful night.

But this dramatic event tore into the fabric of a community in which everyone was related to everyone else, and everyone, whether they liked it or not, was part of a tight hierarchical social network. So to understand the event and its implications we have to create a sense of place and time. What was Branscombe like in the 1880s, how did people make a living, and what was their understanding of the world they lived in? We found ourselves drawn into the detail, the particularity, of people's relationships and experiences.

We like the fact that this is a parochial story. People are formed by the places they live in, especially if they live in the same place all their lives. John Clare, the nineteenth-century worker poet who lived in Northamptonshire, only felt comfortable when he wrote 'within his knowledge' – about country scenes and footpaths that were part of his life, and had made him the person he was. Patrick Kavanagh, the Irish poet, wrote: 'the parish is not a perimeter, but an aperture: a space through which the world can be seen, and again, to know fully even one field or one land is a lifetime's experience. … It is depth that counts, not width.' [3]

To recreate this intimate sense of place and belonging, we have used not only archival sources but also oral histories, and perhaps this needs some justification. Obviously, the direct memories of people alive today, or recently alive, cannot reach back to the 1880s. But take Lily Gush, one of the people we quote. She was born in 1901, had personal memories that started in 1904 or 1905, and remembered stories told by her father, Edwin Gush, born in 1863, and her grandfather, William Rendell, born in 1830. So it is quite possible for recent or present-day oral history to touch on something that happened over a hundred and fifty years ago.

We also think that memories of the early twentieth century can illuminate conditions in the late nineteenth. Some aspects of society change quickly, others more slowly. When Horace Pike, born in 1926, recalls an old man knapping flints for house building, or Brian Dowell describes how his father and grandfather repaired the roads, they are describing much older practices. And when Lesley Collier notes the way in which the interconnected top families could make or break a working man or woman, he sheds light on social pressures that certainly prevailed in the late nineteenth century.

Oral histories are often more democratic than official histories. They help us 'to read the sources against the grain, searching out hints of different views of events, and looking for cracks in the conservative story ...' [4] But, interestingly, oral histories are often silent about certain sorts of event that occur in a community. When something is done that is illegal, or perhaps thought to be shameful, people clam up and then the story may get lost. So it was, we suspect, with the shooting and its aftermath — a wall of silence to the outside world, certainly, but also a reticence in remembering or retelling.

Parochial events are always interwoven with much broader historical patterns. Changes in world trade meant that England, at the time we are writing about, was in the middle of a severe economic depression. Branscombe, always a marginal place economically, felt the wind. But like everywhere else, it dealt with it in its own particular way. Farm workers, for instance, were able to grow early potatoes on small cliff plats carved out of coastal landslips, and improved transport allowed them to send their produce to distant markets. Improved transport also made it easier for people to leave and find work in the new industrial centres, or emigrate to the colonies. Meanwhile the Education Act of 1870 meant that every child had to attend school, and the Third Reform Act of 1884 gave the vote to most men (but not to women). These general trends and particular reforms affected everyday life in the village.

Our book, then, is about a local one-off event, but to understand what happened, and why, we have to both explore parochial minutiae and take a broad brush to developments far beyond the parish boundaries.

Telling the story: genesis, sources, and acknowledgements

In September 1992 Kingsley Squire, a Branscombe-born journalist, wrote a piece entitled 'Shotgun blast that blew a village apart' in the *Sidmouth Herald*. He had been inspired by reading a rare surviving copy of William Dean Dowell's pamphlet, recognizing that it not only told a remarkable story, but also opened an unexpected window on village life in Devon in the late nineteenth century.

At about the same time that Kingsley wrote his piece, a small group of people, including one of the authors of the present book, launched the Branscombe Project (see inside cover). The idea was to gather oral accounts, archive material and items of material culture touching on all aspects of Branscombe village life. It has become a community project with annual exhibitions and entertainments, in which the second author, arriving later, has been much involved.

Following Kingsley's newspaper account, the Project wanted to create an exhibition around the Perryman story but found that the Dowell pamphlet had disappeared, its owner having died. Marie Dowell, whose husband Ivor Dowell is related to William Dean Dowell, finally tracked it down in the possession of Robin Somers. It was a great day when the battered and sellotaped pages were finally in our hands (Figure 1, p. 6). On reading, it turned out every bit as good as we had hoped — indeed much better. [5]

Meanwhile, Margaret Lewis at Allhallows Museum, Honiton, who had thought of researching the subject herself, kindly gave us copies of contemporary newspaper reports.

Then came a remarkable contribution from Bill Carpenter, who lives in Branscombe and is in his eighties. He has a formidable

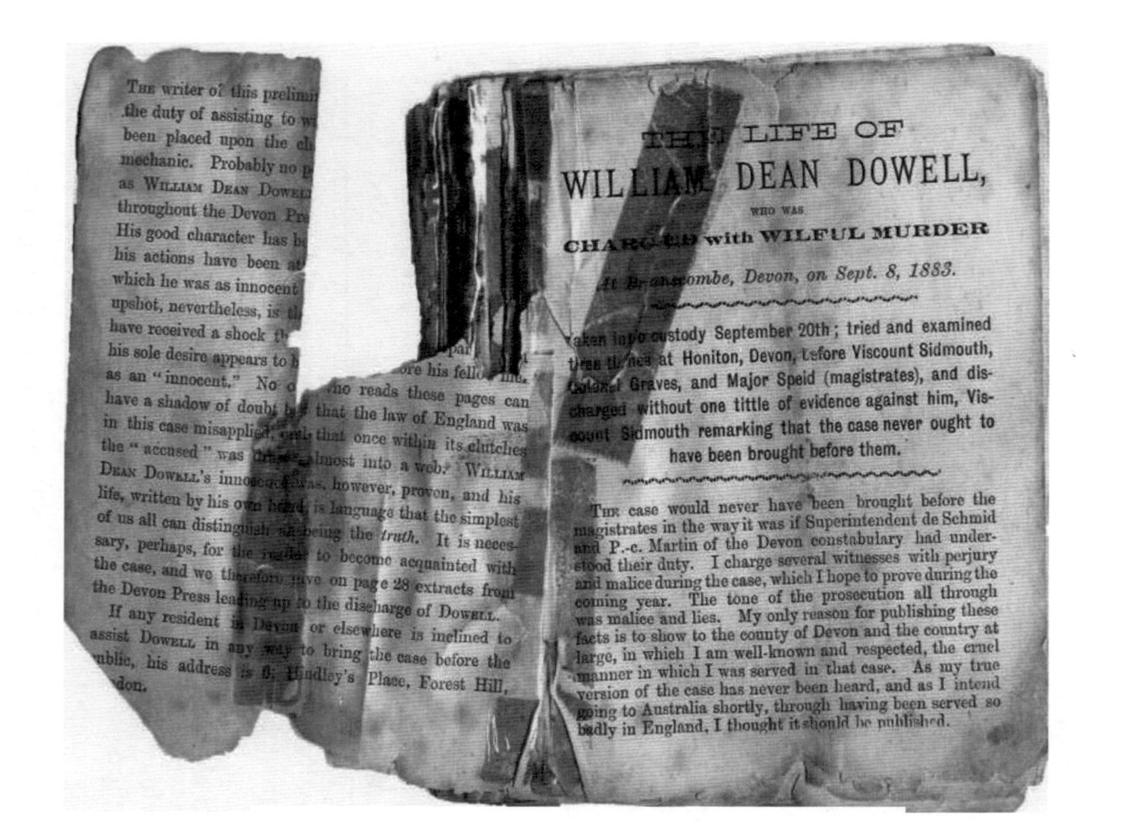

THE LIFE OF

WILLIAM DEAN DOWELL,

WHO WAS

CHARGED with WILFUL MURDER

At Branscombe, Devon, on Sept. 8, 1883.

Taken into custody September 20th; tried and examined three times at Honiton, Devon, before Viscount Sidmouth, Colonel Graves, and Major Speid (magistrates), and discharged without one tittle of evidence against him, Viscount Sidmouth remarking that the case never ought to have been brought before them.

The case would never have been brought before the magistrates in the way it was if Superintendent de Schmid and P.-c. Martin of the Devon constabulary had understood their duty. I charge several witnesses with perjury and malice during the case, which I hope to prove during the coming year. The tone of the prosecution all through was malice and lies. My only reason for publishing these facts is to show to the county of Devon and the country at large, in which I am well-known and respected, the cruel manner in which I was served in that case. As my true version of the case has never been heard, and as I intend going to Australia shortly, through having been served so badly in England, I thought it should be published.

The writer of this prelim…
the duty of assisting to w…
been placed upon the ch…
mechanic. Probably no p…
as William Dean Dowell…
throughout the Devon Pr…
His good character has b…
his actions have been at…
which he was as innocent…
upshot, nevertheless, is th…
have received a shock th…
his sole desire appears to b… …ore his fellow men.
as an "innocent." No o… …ho reads these pages can
have a shadow of doubt … that the law of England was
in this case misapplied, … that once within its clutches
the "accused" was … almost into a web. William
Dean Dowell's innoc… however, proven, and his
life, written by his own hand, is language that the simplest
of us all can distinguish … being the *truth*. It is necessary, perhaps, for the … to become acquainted with
the case, and we therefore give on page 28 extracts from
the Devon Press leading up to the discharge of Dowell.

If any resident in Devon or elsewhere is inclined to
assist Dowell in any way to bring the case before the
…ublic, his address is 6, Hindley's Place, Forest Hill,
…don.

Figure 1. First page of William Dowell's pamphlet

memory and one day he recounted that his great-aunt, Agnes Ward, when in her nineties, had talked to him about the shooting. She told him things that never appeared in the newspapers or in Dowell's pamphlet — things that opened up a completely new line of inquiry.

When we finally got around to researching the story more thoroughly, first for a documentary drama in the village, and then for this book, these three sources — the pamphlet, the newspaper cuttings, and the snippet of oral history — gave us the main outline. The filling-in, as more and more questions emerged, took us in many different directions.

Further study of press coverage of the Branscombe case, of related cases brought before the Honiton magistrates, and of local political activity in the years immediately after the killing, was carried out in the West Country Studies Library and the Devon and Exeter Institution in Exeter, Sidmouth Public Library, the Somerset Record Office at Taunton, and the British Library newspaper archive at Colindale.

Censuses and parish registers were the main source of information about births, deaths and marriages in the village, and thus about its tightly knit kin network. Databases of censuses and registers, compiled by Dan Ponsford for the Project, have been invaluable. Birth and death certificates, obtained from the General Registry Office, confirmed details of illegitimacies and suicides. We have also drawn on family trees of the Dowells, compiled by Ivor and Marie Dowell's daughter, Dawn Squire; of the French family, compiled by Margaret Lewis; and of other village families compiled by David Rockey. Sid Sweetland and John Bass lent us material about the French family. Tanya and Rae Cload gave us information and photos of the Williams family.

The Devon Record Office in Exeter provided details of the inmates of Exminster Asylum, and of those given outdoor relief or workhouse accommodation by the Honiton Poor Law Union in the 1880s. Records of Petty and Quarter sessions were also consulted in the D.R.O., as were the well-indexed holdings of Ford family papers. We also found relevant material in a trunk of Ford family documents held by Henry Ford's collateral descendant, Perry Tucker.

The National Archives at Kew provided background on Superintendent de Schmid of the Honiton police, from army lists, the history of the Devon Regiment, and his naturalization papers.

Through the internet we were able to contact Jane Harris, a descendant of William Dean Dowell, who passed on to us a copy of a poignant letter written by him, with a family tradition about its context. The open-ended resources accessed through Google were, of course, a fount of information, both general and particular.

The Branscombe Project's own oral history archive provided much detail on village life. Going back to it, we found, to our sorrow, that many of the people we cite in this book have since died – Wynne Clarke, Lesley Collier, Lily Gush, Horace Pike, Phoebe Spencer and Laura Somers.

When we 'footstepped' the path taken by John Perryman, trying to pinpoint where he was killed and to trace the possible escape paths of his killer, or when we reconstructed the stretch of village road that figured in William Dowell's alibi, we used various maps. The 1889 Ordnance Survey first of all, but also the 1840 tithe map, digitized by Philip Planel for the AONB East Devon Parishscapes Project. We were further helped by Bill and Eileen Carpenter's memories of the terrain, and by Celia Andrews, whose steep garden led us to an overgrown footpath. Sue Brewer, who lives next door to the house where William Dowell lived in 1883, showed us architectural features and documents that illuminated the story.

Elsie Mayo who holds the Branscombe Parish Council photo archive provided much help with photographs. And when, rather late, we discovered how much could be gleaned from old village postcards, Peter Simkins and Geoffrey Squire allowed us to use their comprehensive collections. These gave us a much better sense of how the village looked at the end of the nineteenth century, and showed us pastures, paths and allotments no longer visible.

General acknowledgements

Our thanks go to all the people and institutions mentioned in the Preface; also to Phil Planel for information, advice, and wide-ranging discussions; Sue Clifford and Angela King of Common Ground for always stressing local particularity; Sue Dymond for ferreting out important bits of information; Joan Doern for much help with layout and illustrations; Rodney Lyons, Mike Bender, Rowland Molony and Marjorie Williams, who read the book in draft and made many acute and helpful suggestions. Our special thanks go to Cory Lyons for her marvellous pictures.

INTRODUCTION

Branscombe, Early 1880s

> *George Chaloner:* If a reader ... desires perfect rest for a space, let him go to Branscombe. There is no one there to talk to except the natives; nothing to excite, nothing even to look at but the hills, the valleys, and the sea. He may gather watercresses in the brook; catch butterflies in the fields; pick blackberries on the sides of the cliffs; may even lie on the beach for hours in perfect solitude. There are no visitors, and there is no society. Dress as you please, do as you like, none can say you nay. [1]

Chaloner, a Methodist printer, was writing in 1871. Some years earlier he had been ill, and Branscombe's beauty and tranquillity had restored him to health. Naturally enough, he presented an outsider's idealised view. Twenty-seven years later, in 1898, the travel writer W. H. Hudson, was equally ecstatic and uncritical. Branscombe was beginning to be discovered, and he noted that visitors were treated with kindness, and that since there was no space in the overcrowded cottages, they were given beds in hay-lofts and out-houses. Hudson recounted how walking towards Branscombe on a hot day, he stopped off at a hamlet to ask for a drink. Being a susceptible fellow, he was transfixed by the beauty of the young mother, breast-feeding her baby, who offered him water. When he mentioned that he was going to Branscombe, her face lit up:

> "Its my home! I was born there ...." She went on to tell me that Branscombe was such a dear, queer, funny old place ... People that went there sometimes laughed at first, because it was such a funny, tumbledown old place; but they always said afterwards that there was no such sweet spot. [2]

She and her husband were villagers, born and bred, and she loved, and missed, her home. But reading between the lines, it is

Plate 1. Branscombe Mouth

Plate 2. The Masons Arms at Vicarage

Plate 3. St. Winifred's church

Plate 4. Street

clear that there was not enough work to be had in the village, and they had had to leave.

Setting the scene

In this introduction we want to take you back a hundred and thirty years to the 1880s, to create a sense of place and belonging. Those who live in the village will have to re-imagine familiar places and a very different way of life. And for those who do not know Branscombe, we want not only to go back in time but to give you a sense of its topography so that you can picture more vividly the story as it unfolds (Figure 2, p. 12).

Imagine, if you are coming by sea, a long pebble beach, a valley with a little river running into the pebbles, white chalk cliffs and tall stacks to the east, red cliffs to the west. This is Branscombe Mouth (Plate 1). There are a few two-masted fishing luggers drawn up on the shingle, and a number of small rowing boats. On the beach there is a defunct gypsum mill and, further back, a stone-walled coal-yard where Welsh anthracite ('culm'), landed by boat, used to be stored for use in the lime kilns.[3]

Part way up the cliff on the western side, there is a long low row of coastguard cottages still occupied by the families of the preventive officers. But smuggling has become less profitable because of the reduction in Customs duties and the improvement of the coastguard service. Only the occasional cask of high-proof brandy is still brought in illegally, and the spirit watered and sold. Except for a glimpse of a barn, no other buildings are visible.

Inland there is a completely different scene. Imagine that you are coming by road, in a horse-drawn vehicle or on foot. The turnpike road from Lyme Regis to Sidmouth is in fairly good shape, and runs across a high flinty clay plateau with rectangular arable fields on either side. You might stop to take refreshment at The Three Horseshoes inn, but very few will turn off on to the rough lanes leading south to Branscombe and the sea.

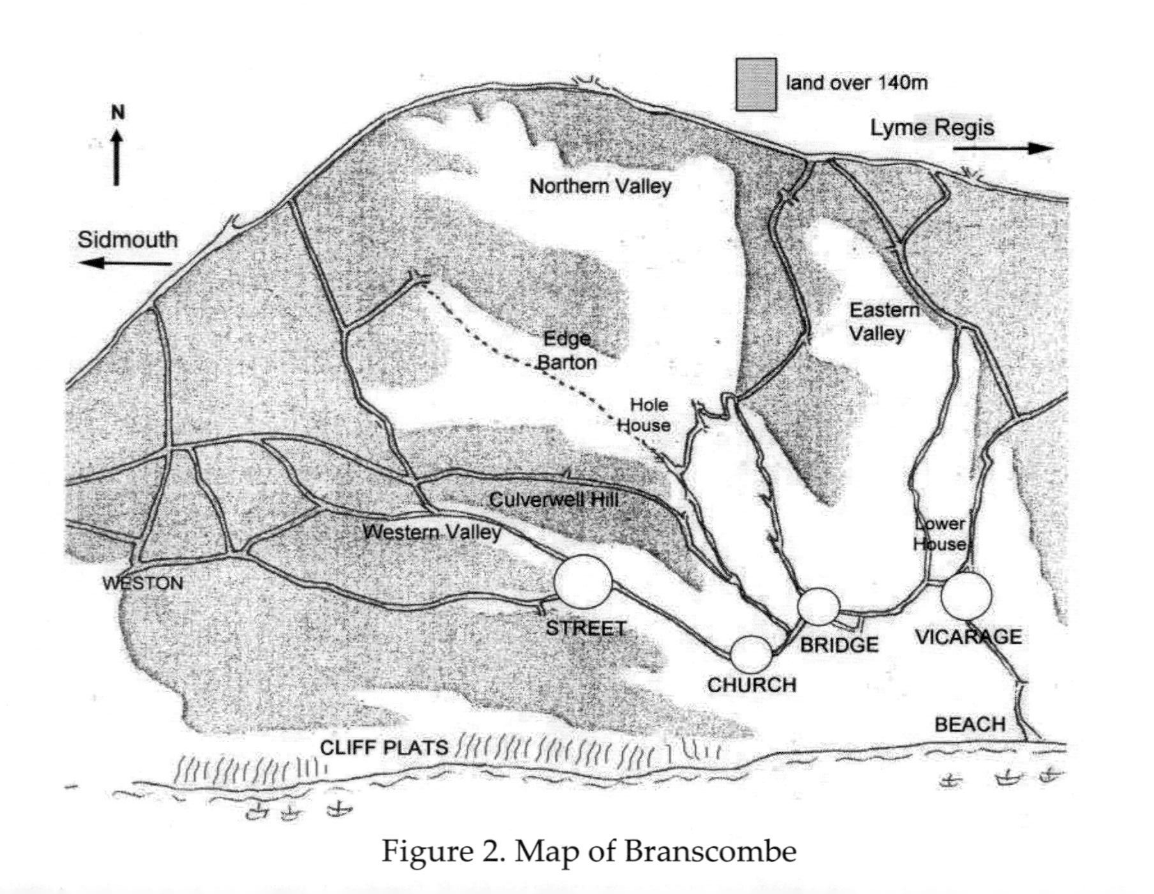

Figure 2. Map of Branscombe

If you do turn off, you find that the lanes quickly descend into steep-sided valleys with tiny, irregular hedged fields. There are three such valleys – the eastern, northern and western valleys, of which the northern (central) valley is the largest. The three valleys coalesce about a mile from the coast, and their streams unite to form a small river that runs to the sea through a narrow floodplain with water meadows. The scenery is more open, less wooded than today, but some of the hilltops are covered with scrub and bramble and a few trees. Beneath the scrubby woodland are numerous small quarries and pits that were once used to extract building-stone or sand, chalk for lime-burning, and flint for building, road-mending and flint-lock guns. You may see the odd lime-kiln with associated dumps of waste flint and trackways and turning places for horse-drawn carts, but nearly all these sites have gone out of use and are becoming overgrown.

A dear, queer, funny old place

The village consists of two main clusters of houses, perhaps originally two hamlets, over a mile apart.

'Vicarage' (now 'Square') is at the eastern end, 'Street' at the western. Two smaller clusters — 'Bridge' and 'Church' — lie between them. Another hamlet, Weston, lies still further west, close to the parish boundary.

Bridge

'Vicarage' is low down at the mouth of the eastern valley, out of sight of the sea and earlier sea-borne marauders. There is an inn, The Masons Arms (Plate 2), which some say was named for the masons that used to work across the hill in the Beer quarries, and almost opposite stands the old vicarage itself with its long, walled glebe land running south beside Parsons Lane.

The main village road, which runs west from Vicarage, rises and dips again to Bridge, where the northern and western valleys meet, and where there is a smithy, a mill and a bakery, and then climbs on up through Church towards Street. On the northern, sunny side of the road are terraced cottages, and a little way above them, up School Lane, the windows of the new church school glint in the sun.

Halfway between Vicarage and Street, as if trying to unite the two halves of the village, stands the fine old church of St Winifred's, set back south of the road (Plate 3). The church, though well attended, is in poor repair, and the churchyard is a disgrace:

> [This churchyard] is a gruesome place – a veritable Golgotha. On every grave ... evidences of human mortality may be picked up by the handful. Bones of every shape and size stare one full in the face, from the small bones of the child up to portions of the thick skull-pan of the seventy-year-old. The ground is literally gorged with human remains .... Conversing afterwards with a villager ... he said ... 'What can be done when the place is chock full? It's a case then of "Tommy make room for your uncle."' The grave-digger in Hamlet could hardly have put the case more sententiously. [4]

The church authorities have finally agreed to extend the churchyard, and some small houses close to the church are being pulled down to make room.

Continuing uphill towards Street, you pass more terraced cottages on the north side of the road with names like Upper Church, Grapevine and Blue Ball. Behind them are steep fields, some given over to allotments, which slope up towards a scrubby hillside riddled with old quarries. This is the south flank of Culverwell Hill, and both terraced houses and hill figure largely in our story. [5]

So, finally, you reach Street (Plate 4), a compact cluster of houses with its own pub, The Fountain Head (Plate 9), another smithy, and a small but flourishing Methodist chapel.

The big houses

There used to be several big houses in the village, but most of these (Edge Barton, Hole House, Higher House, Margels) have seen better times and are now occupied by tenant farmers. Barnells, still owner-occupied, sits high on the hillside above Bridge. It was built by a veteran of Trafalgar and more recently enlarged by the tight-fisted lace-manufacturer John Tucker. He had a monopoly on lace-making in the village and forced the lace-makers to buy their provisions at the truck-shop [6] which he built alongside the house, in part-payment for their work. But even before Tucker died in 1877 lace-making was in decline, and once he had gone his four unmarried daughters locked up the hated workshop. [7] Even so the village women still earn a bit of money by making small lace pieces to sell to the occasional visitor, or at the corner shop at Street, or the Lace Shop in the neighbouring village of Beer.

The other big house, Lower House, belongs to Henry Ford. Built on rather low-lying land in the eastern valley, it is gloomy and damp. But the Fords have become the most important family in the village, having made money from lime-burning at Beer. In 1864 Henry united the two big families by marrying John Tucker's eldest daughter Mary. Shortly afterwards he bought the lordship of the manor and many of the farms from the Dean and Chapter of Exeter Cathedral and established himself as village squire. He is now in his forties, and is setting up a company to revive the once-famous stone quarry at Beer.

This enterprising, rather bullying man plays a significant role in our story. William Dean Dowell, our 'hero', the man accused of murder, portrays him as the archetypal oppressive landlord, and the Reverend Robert Swansborough, the vicar, as his crony:

Henry Ford

Rev. Swansborough

'Mr Ford (that's the bloke who has got nearly all the land in the village,) ... [and the Reverend Swansborough] these two are rulers supreme there amongst the poor ignorant mortals, but, thank God, the rising generation will have more sense, as they go to school there now.' [8]

Dowell, in spite of his bitterness, is a valuable witness. Unlike the visiting outsiders with their starry-eyed gaze, he knew the village intimately and had good reason to expose its darker sides.

Farming

The most striking thing about the village is the number of small farms (twenty, where now there are only four). More than half of them are less that 200 acres in size, and only one, Edge Farm, is over 300 acres. All the farms are rented, and apart from Henry Ford the owners are absentee landlords. It is mostly mixed farming — beef and dairy cattle and sheep graze the small hedged pastures on the slopes, with arable on the flat land above the village. Alongside each farmhouse there is an acre or two of orchard, bright with apple-blossom in the spring (Plate 5). 'Pretty as a picture', but the reality is that farming these stony uplands and steep valleys has always been marginal, and is becoming more so. The farms are too small to take advantage of the new mechanization, and agricultural prices have been depressed by imports of cheap wheat from North America.

Both farmers and labourers feel the squeeze, but the farmers at least have status within the community — they are rate-payers, they form the parish council (or Vestry) and influence local affairs When, out of the blue, a man is shot dead and an inquest has to be held in the village, it is they who mainly compose the jury. (See Appendix A.)

In contrast, the farm-workers are really up against it. Fewer men are being employed on the farms, their already meagre wages are

Plate 5. Apple picking at Weston

Plate 6. Lace-makers and cliff plat farmers outside Grapevine

Plate 7. Cliff plats under near Branscombe Mouth

Plate 8. Cliff plat donkeys with crubs

under threat, and the fact that overtime is paid in cider, not cash, makes things worse rather than better. Here is Dowell again, waxing indignant on their behalf:

> I felt for them in their oppression, as they work very hard for the enormous sum of 10s. per week. … If there is a bad season, who has to suffer through it? You labourers, or the rich landlords? … When I left last September [1884] they were thinking of dropping the wages because there was no price for their corn. Shameful! Why didn't the farmers compel the landlord to drop their rent instead of making all the little children in the village suffer, as he could well afford to lower it by half? No! they are afraid. [9]

Do you think Dowell is exaggerating? Times are so hard that a man may be up before the bench for stealing turnips.[10] Typical weekly expenditure on food staples, lamp oil and candles by a working rural family has been reckoned at 19s 9d. That's without rent, clothing and shoes. And yet a Branscombe labourer earns only 10s a week, while a young son working on a farm might bring in another 7s. Seventeen shillings in all – it is clear that by the end of a week a large family only just scrapes by. (See Appendix A.)

Scraping by

By the 1880s most sources of livelihood in Branscombe — lime-burning, lace-making, and farming — are in decline. But one small, laborious but minutely profitable industry is growing: raising early potatoes and vegetables on tiny cliff plats carved out of the land-slips east and west of Branscombe Mouth (Plates 7 and 8). Here W. H. Hudson describes the scene:

> The patches, wildly irregular in form, some on such steeply sloping ground as to suggest the idea that they must have been cultivated on all fours, are divided from each other by ridges and by masses of rock … The effect was very singular; the huge rough mass of jumbled rock and soil … and, scattered irregularly about its surface, the plots … of cultivated smoothness - potato rows like parallel lines ruled

> on a grey ground, and big, blue-green, equidistant cabbage-globes — each plot with its fringe of spike-like onion leaves, crinkled parsley, and other garden herbs.[11]

These south-facing slopes form a frost-free micro-environment, and now that roads have improved and steam trains are opening up markets, the early produce can be sent on its way to the cities.

It is hard work bringing seaweed up from the seashore by donkey to fertilise the potato beds, carrying back the soil that slips downslope (foreheading), lifting the crops, then loading up donkeys and leading them by precipitous paths to the cliff-tops and home again, but it gives the farm labourers who rent the plots a small extra income and a sort of independence. Not long before, the same paths were used for smuggling, and some who worked plats by day hid contraband there at night.

Farm workers, cliff-plat farmers, artisans and the odd fisherman or lime-burner rent the terraced cottages which belong to Henry Ford or other landlords. There are 850 inhabitants in the village (where today there are less than 450, many of them second-homers) and yet there are fewer houses than now.[12] Families are much larger, so you have to double, treble, or quadruple the number of people occupying each small dwelling. Children often sleep away from home with relatives or friends who have a little more space. Even so, where possible, people use their small front rooms or sheds for non-domestic purposes. The front room may serve as a shop, or a cobbler or tailor may ply his trade. Women make their lace. Men often have more than one trade: the man who works the forge delivers the letters and sweeps the chimneys, the landlord of one pub is a carpenter and coffin-maker, and the landlord of the other is also a butcher — any combination that brings in extra money.

Daily life

The cottagers have no money to spend on their surroundings, and they move quite frequently from one tumbledown village house to another. Henry Ford and the other landlords, some of whom are village tradesmen, have little interest in improvements, so the terraces and houses remain unpainted, poorly thatched and damp.[13] Inside, though there is very little furniture, the women try to keep things neat and tidy. Respectability is important.

The privies, of course, are outside, often over streams (the watercress downstream is particularly luxuriant). Water is fetched from wells, pumps and spring-water shutes. [14] These, with the streams, supply all the water for households, donkeys, pigs, poultry and allotments. They are also meeting-places where particularly the women can gather, pass the time of day and exchange news and gossip.

Village life is very different from today — far more people, many more animals, a quite different range of smells and noises. Alongside or behind the houses are stone-built linhays (sheds) for donkeys or for storing potatoes, and also pig-sties, poultry runs, gardens and allotments. During the daytime, women and children are constantly on the move — to well or allotment, visiting neighbours, buying small items from one of the small shops or a bit of fish from someone who has just come through the village with his catch. The roads are rough, and clapped-out boots must often be taken to one of the several cobblers to put on yet another patch or set of studs. As recalled by Horace Pike, a more recent villager remembering his childhood:

> We kids was allowed a pair of boots about once a year. You bought your boots at the beginning o' the winter, and worn 'em when they were good through the winter, and by the end of the summer your toes were sticking out! But you still wore 'em! [15]

In fine weather women sit outside with their lace-work (Plate 6). There is a bit of interest when once in a while a nob rattles past in a carriage, or the carrier's cart plods through, or the grocer's or tinker's cart comes by. There may be news from the outside world, letters to be pored over and deciphered from sons who have gone away, and maybe a small remittance to rejoice over. News of births and deaths in the neighbourhood will quickly go the rounds, for the older women are both midwives to the newborn and layers-out of the dead.[16] And there will be talk about who is in the family way and sometimes a whispered interest in who the father might be; a shaking of heads over neighbours and relatives who have had to go on Poor Law relief, or have been sent to the asylum, and worry when yet another man has been fined for not sending his children to school, or jailed for a bit of poaching.

Later in the day, when the men get back from the fields or plats and have eaten, they loiter outside in dry weather, smoking and talking. Here once again, is W. H. Hudson:

> The men were mostly farm labourers, and after their day's work they would sit out-of-doors on the ground to smoke their pipes; and where the narrow crooked little street was narrowest – at my end of the village, when two men would sit opposite each other, each at his own door, with legs stretched out before them, their boots would very nearly touch in the middle of the road ... When daylight faded the village was very dark – no lamp for the visitors – and very silent ... [17]

Or men will make their way up, or down, to one of the inns. As the beer is drawn and the clay pipes lit, it is their turn to ruminate on the day's events or news from outside. There may be music-making and story-telling. Voices, whether men or women, sound different from today, softer and rising at the end of each sentence. There are phrases and jokes that we would not understand, [18] and no urgency in the telling of a tale. Here, at a later date, is how Horace Pike describes a scene:

> Up the top of Culverwell, you go through the cross gate, and on your left there used to be seven 'olly trees. An' ... they used to bring the stones out of the quarry which is up that wheel track just to the side of the wood. They used to bring it down there, an' this old man, I don't know who 'e was, used to crack 'em with a piece o' stick with a fork on the end, and a 'ammer and 'is pair o' old wire knitting glasses, and 'e used to crack the stones, an' the stones 'ad to be of a certain size. And that was what the fork was – that was the width of the stone. 'E used to 'aul 'em down and crack, crack, haul 'em down and

crack, crack, and then pack 'em ... in a yard be a yard — 'e used to pack 'is stones up in a square lump. [19]

Generally people go early to bed, because light means burning candles or kerosene lamps, both of which are expensive. As Dowell sourly remarks:

> All the poor slaves can do after they leave work in the evening, is to go to the public [house] if they have a copper to spend, or go to bed. [20]

A few men, however, may still be out under cover of darkness, setting snares and traps or carrying a poacher's gun. Couples too may be out on fine evenings — most children are conceived before the banns are read. There are also occasional attempts to molest young women in the dark.

Church, chapel and superstition

John & Jane Ward at Grapevine

Sunday is the only day off, and the only time the family have together, much of it spent in church, chapel or Sunday school. Elijah Chick, the Branscombe-born village historian, says: 'A walk of a mile, or a mile and a half, in each direction twice or three times on the Sabbath was cheerfully undertaken'. [21]

Until the coming of the elementary school in 1878, there were only a couple of dame schools in the village where for a penny or so children might get a bit of education. Failing that, the Methodist Sunday school was the only chance of learning to read and write.

Times are hard, chances for getting on are few, and village life can be stifling. There is church and chapel, and there is also a great deal of superstition. Elijah Chick writes, rather benignly, of an old lady who is a fervent chapel-goer: 'Probably as deep set as her religion was her belief in the realities of witchcraft, shared by most of her contemporaries'. He goes on to recount an incident:

> A gentleman of the neighbourhood had on the sea-beach a small boat from which the oars were stolen. Repeated enquiries failed to discover the culprit or to secure the return of the oars. In despair my friend declared he would go to the white witch at Exeter. Terror took the place of bravado, and next day found the oars in their proper place.

Another story tells of an over-zealous coastguard who, a little earlier in the nineteenth century, was found dead at the foot of the cliff:

> Some said that he had partaken too freely of the "still-liquors" [distilled cider]. Others swore that he had been "witched" by old granny White who had made a mommet (straw doll) of him or that he had stepped into one of her magic circles drawn in the dusty road near the church. [22]

Dowell, as is his wont, is less tolerant:

> Most of the people in Branscombe are very ignorant and superstitious, and believe very much in witchcraft. If they are taken ill and don't get well quick they say they are bewitched, and then they will give pounds to an old man that pretends to cure these things. [23]

No doubt superstition also plays a part in the strange, rather lurid events that sometimes occur around Guy Fawkes' night. In many neighbouring towns and villages — Sidmouth,[24] Axmouth, Colyton, Ottery, Topsham, Woodbury, to mention a few — November 5th is a night of lawless disorder, a time for bonfires and fireballs and burning tar barrels, and for gangs of masked men taking revenge on people by setting fire to their establishments. In some places, including Branscombe, revenge sometimes takes the form of burning an effigy of the victim. In the course of our story we describe two such occasions — both very frightening.

Leaving home

For many younger men the only way to get on is to get out. Some go to America, some go to Wales and work down the mines. Others set off to one of the big towns where there is plenty of work to be had building factories, back-to-backs, public institutions and churches. William Dean Dowell is one of those who have left home, which is why, when he comes back, he looks at his fellow villagers with a more critical eye.

PART ONE

THE NIGHT OF THE SHOOTING

CHAPTER ONE

Shot by Moonlight

Between eight and nine o'clock on a warm September evening — September 8th, 1883, to be exact — seven labourers are walking back to Branscombe after a long days harvesting in some outlying fields.[1] The fields are on the high level ground that rims the village to the north, and belong to Edge Farm. Although it is Saturday, the men have worked until long after sunset to get the harvest in before the weather breaks, and now a full moon lights their way home.

Three of the men — John Perryman, Robert Loveridge and Thomas Newton — walk on together while a fourth, William Bartlett, stays behind to collect firewood. The last three, David Pile, John Pile and Samuel Wyatt, follow on a little later.

John Perryman is 67. He still has to work — a farm worker's wage allows no saving for retirement — but for the time being he is fit enough. His wife Sarah is older and infirm, but she still manages to keep house and does a little lace-making. The two men with him are a good deal younger. As they walk along they talk a little — Loveridge later recalls the conversation as being 'of an ordinary description'. Perhaps they are looking forward to Farmer Pyle's Harvest Feast in a couple of weeks' time.

The walk to the village from Edge Farm is just over a mile. The track skirts the northern side of Culverwell Hill, a long spur of high ground separating the northern valley from the western valley which contains the straggling village. Soon after passing Hole House, Perryman and Loveridge say goodnight to Newton and turn off to the right. Newton keeps on down, past Culverwell Farm into School Lane, past the new school, and comes out on the village street below the church. There he turns left, downhill, to his cottage at Bridge.

Meanwhile Perryman and Loveridge climb up the small steep path through Hole Coppice. They live at the upper end of the village, and their quickest way home is to walk over the top of Culverwell Hill and down the other side. The coppice path comes out at Windwhistle Gate on Northern Lane, higher up the hillside, and from here a track swings round towards the hilltop through a scarred landscape of old quarries and pits. [2]

Another short steep climb brings them to the top of the hill, where a stile leads into a wide field hummocked with old pits. [3] The track ahead of them, known as Pit Lane, crosses the field and then drops down between hedgebanks, coming out opposite The Fountain Head Inn on Street. Loveridge lives at Street and this is his way home. But Perryman lives further down the village towards the church, so just after the stile he usually takes a short cut, turning left on to a rough footpath through a dense cluster of pits known simply as Old Pits. This will take him out on to steep fields above two terraces of thatched cottages, Blue Ball and Grapevine. Grapevine is where he lives.

This evening, as usual, the two men bid each other goodnight near the stile and Perryman turns off. It is hard going among the gorse-bushes and pits, which the moonlight turns into an eerie black and white landscape, but he knows the path and strides along easily enough. He is almost out of the pits, coming up over the last bank, when a gun suddenly blasts off in front of him. He takes the charge full in the chest and stomach. Mortally wounded, he staggers a few steps, falls, and cries out for help.

His cries are heard by two men walking along the village street below. They race up the path that he would have taken, and guided by his groans they find him lying on his side. He still has strength enough to murmur a few words, but when they try to lift him blood pours from his mouth. They shout for assistance and are shortly joined by a young man who helps to carry him down to Grapevine, but by the time they bring him in to where Sarah Perryman is waiting, he is dead.

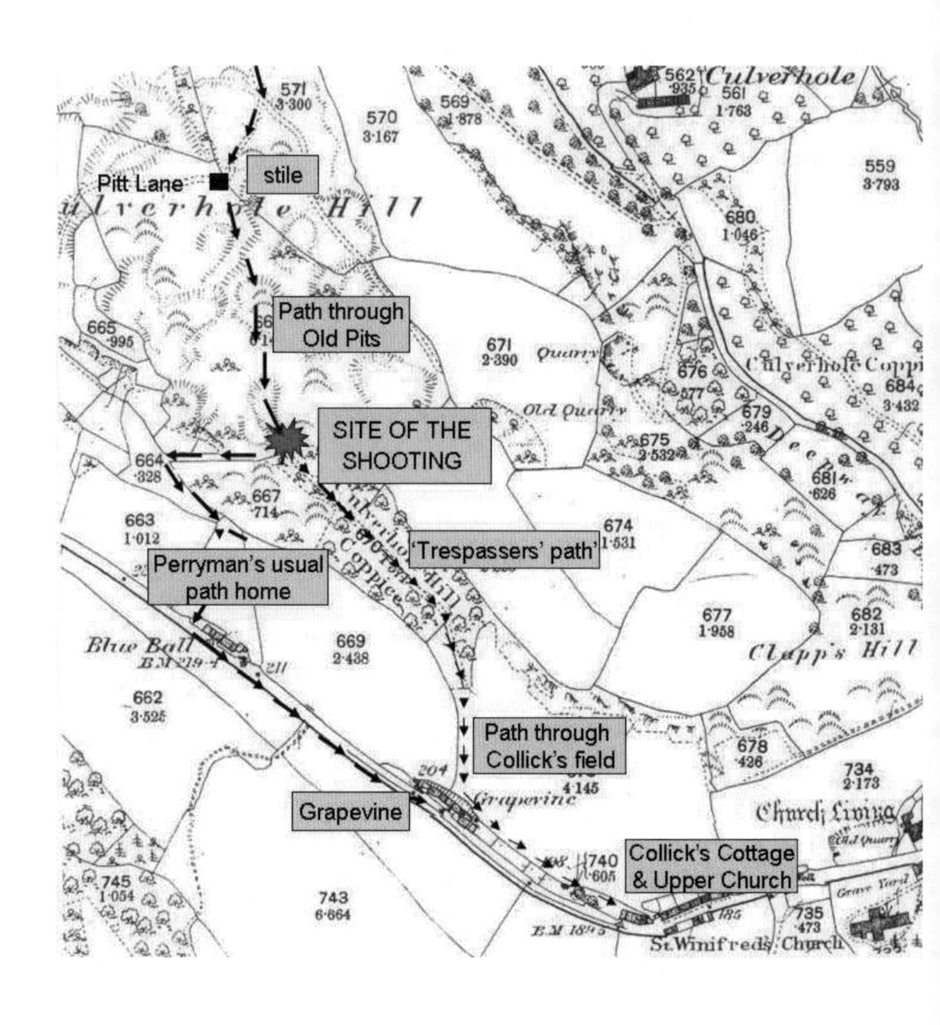

Figure 3: Perryman's way home and the site of the shooting

CHAPTER TWO

The Victim

Chapel man

Bewilderment and consternation greeted the news of John Perryman's death. At the inquest which followed witness after witness said they had never known him to quarrel with anyone, and no one could believe him to be the intended victim of a murder. He was a much-loved elder of the Methodist congregation in Branscombe, and Richard Lethaby, editor of *Lethaby's Sidmouth Journal* and himself a Methodist, wrote:

> The Wesleyan Sunday school at Branscombe has, for more than half a century, been celebrated for its vigour and success; one generation succeeding another, as the child developed into the parent, and so carried on a sort of family succession, of which all parties were justly proud. At the head of that school, officiating as its Superintendent for more than two score years, and consequently lovingly regarded by old and young, was a zealous cheerful labouring man, John Perryman by name, 68 years old, who had a kindly word and a beaming smile for everybody, and was as much respected as though he had wealth and high social position. [1]

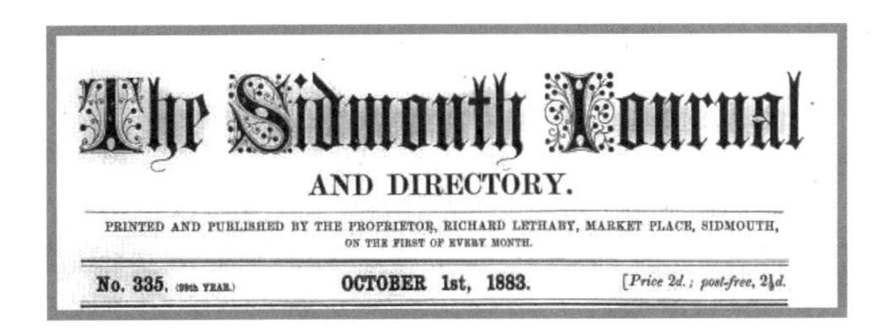

The Sidmouth Journal

AND DIRECTORY.

PRINTED AND PUBLISHED BY THE PROPRIETOR, RICHARD LETHABY, MARKET PLACE, SIDMOUTH, ON THE FIRST OF EVERY MONTH.

No. 335. OCTOBER 1st, 1883. [Price 2d.; post-free, 2½d.

THE CHAPEL

The first Methodist society was formed in Branscombe in 1815. At first meetings were held in people's houses, including Samuel and Abigail Chick's farmhouse at Berry Barton. By 1832 there were 24 members, and a chapel was built in Street. It was a small stone building with a thatched roof, and had a gallery for the musicians. It is now a private dwelling but still has a stone over the doorway announcing its original purpose. It was here that John Perryman held his Sunday school. [2]

Elijah Chick describes the evangelical fervour of the old Methodist chapel: *Oh, the twirls of the flute and clarionet, the groanings of the bassoon, or the rattlings of the bass! ... Then the verve of the singing! Why, thirty years ago [early 1870s], in that country congregation, there were six or eight good round bass voices, a splendid groundwork for trebles galore.* [3]

George Chaloner too remembered *The melodious accompaniment to the human voice produced by a bass viol, a concertina, and two asthmatic flutes.*

Lethaby went on to quote a heartfelt eulogy from the *Exeter Flying Post* written by the Reverend Henry Tomkins:

> **I wish to say that his life was a blessing to the whole large parish, for among my 900 parishioners there was not one more useful in good Christian work than the quiet "labourer," John Perryman. He was Superintendent of the Wesleyan Sunday School, diligent, unwearied, cheerful in every good word and work within his reach: a labourer indeed for our heavenly Master. From the day of my entering on my work until the day of my departure, there was no man whose kindly, earnest sympathy and moral support I more valued than good John Perryman.**

John Perryman was clearly a remarkable man, and a remarkably good man, and we catch other glimpses of him in a chapel context. Elijah Chick remembered Perryman's deep Devon voice as prayer leader ('Oh, what a pedal bass!') and recalled that he and his brother James were known as 'Praise-God Boanerges' — 'sons of thunder', the nickname that Jesus gave to his disciples James and John. George Chaloner, a keen butterfly-collector, tells another story which can be traced to Perryman:

> On the third Sunday the Superintendent laid hold of me in one of my moments of weakness, and sent me into the pulpit. I only hope he was satisfied: I can certify that the children got more natural history of me that afternoon than is usually considered proper to a Sunday school. [4]

For many people in the village, Perryman was the man who had taught them to read and write.

> *Dowell*: He had done more good in that village than any other man, for there are a great many young men there now that never would have been able to read, had it not been for the Sunday school ... He was also the first man that taught me to read. [5]

The two young men who went to Perryman's aid would have recognised his voice because they too had been among 'his Sunday school scholars'. [6]

A labouring man

What do we know of John Perryman's life outside the chapel? He was christened at Branscombe on 4 February 1816, the twelfth and youngest child of Isaac Perryman, a labourer, and his wife Jenny Farrant. Born sixteen years from the beginning of the century and killed sixteen years before its end, he lived through a period of great changes, none of which had made life easier for farm workers. His parents had lived to a ripe age, dying at eighty when John was in his early thirties, but at least four of his siblings died young, and by 1883 it seems the only survivors locally were John and his elder brother James. By then James was a widower of 79; he had buried five of his seven children, and had suffered the loss of a hand (he was remembered as 'the man with a hook'). In 1881 he was acting as postman, and also received 4s 6d a week in outdoor relief from the Honiton Poor Law Union. [7]

John married Sarah French in 1835, when he was only nineteen and she twenty-six. They had two sons and two daughters. In 1851 they were living at Pound Tenements, a row of cottages at Street. They were poor – their three oldest children, two boys and a girl, aged 15, 12 and 9 were all working as lace-makers. The youngest, Tamzin, aged 6, was already a servant. Four years later the younger boy, John, died, aged 16. The oldest boy, Robert, married at nineteen, settled near his parents in Street and stayed in the village all his life, working as a farm labourer.

By 1861 John and Sarah had moved to Blue Ball, and by 1865 both daughters, Mary Ann and Tamzin, had married and left home. By 1871 they had moved again, this time to a cottage below the church. They shared it with Mary Ann and her two daughters, because her husband George Clark had joined the Navy. But by 1881, George had become a coastguard and his family had gone to join him at Studland in Dorset, so they were on their own. They had moved to Grapevine, where, two doors down, John's brother James lodged with his son Ephraim and family. [8]

Ephraim Perryman, John's nephew, was a tailor, and another staunch Methodist — he played the bass viol (a precursor of the cello) in the chapel gallery. As a boy he and his brother had been involved in smuggling, and he related his memories to the antiquarian J.Y.A. Morshead in 1893:

> I did little except carrying at 3s. a night, but pay varied with luck, once I made 4s. [Compare with 10s a week for a farm-worker!] My brother was landing tobacco from a vessel … at Lillacombe, when the coast-guard boat rowed out gently from the shadow of the cliffs and took her. 3 men were in the dinghy landing the goods & hearing the noise they turned round & rowed smack out to sea, that was Friday night, & by Sunday afternoon they had rowed to Jersey and sent the goods back to the conveyors. I call that acting honest. [9]

In passing he noted that 'It's not true that Methodists were the worst smugglers. Church and chapel was all one on the beach'. Although a smuggling motive for killing John Perryman can be discounted, it is as well to remember that within his lifetime Branscombe was a village with a secret and sometimes violent nocturnal shadow-life, which had bound together not just church and chapel but squire, vicar, farmer and labourer.

It is clear that John Perryman's life had been a struggle. Like many other farm labourers he rented a cliff plat, but it was a small one. His usual rent was 18s a year, but in 1883, the year in which he died, he paid only half his rent because half his plat had slipped down the cliff.

The Perrymans would not have been able to afford a stone memorial for John. But so much was he loved, and so horrified were the villagers by his violent death, that chapel members and other well-wishers subscribed to give him a fine headstone in the churchyard (See Chapter 17). Inscribed on it is one of his favourite sayings — prophetic, as it turned out — 'Sudden death, sudden glory!' [10]

CHAPTER THREE

Later the Same Night

The news spreads

Evidence given later at the inquest and before the magistrates gives a vivid impression of how swiftly news of the shooting spread that Saturday night.

Shortly after Perryman and his fellow workers had left Edge Farm, they were followed, at about twenty to nine, by David Pile, John Pile, and Samuel Wyatt. [1] David Pile will appear as an important witness later, and is a major figure in the story. It is not known by which routes John Pile and Sam Wyatt went home, but David Pile

> went home by the main road [i.e. down School Lane and up the village road to Upper Church], arriving there about a quarter past nine o'clock. ... He did not enter his cottage because as he came to the drinking well in the village he met Loveridge, who said "David, it is a bad job; someone has shot poor old John Perryman on the Pits". [2]

Robert Loveridge, who had left John Perryman on Culverwell Hill, arrived home at about nine and, in consequence of what he heard, he went to Perryman's cottage. The news must have reached Street extremely fast, for he arrived at Grapevine in time to see William Tidwell, William Williams and Ephraim Perryman carrying John Perryman's dead body into his cottage. [3]

Loveridge continued down the street and met David Pile at the well. This must have been the well which old maps show in the road near Upper Church cottages, where Pile lived (see map, p. 125), but which has since been tarmacked over. It may have been Loveridge's voice that was heard by Pile's next-door neighbour Eliza Williams, for she heard someone outside her house speaking to David Pile.

She heard them say 'John Perryman is shot'. [4] She immediately went down the terrace to tell her neighbours, Amos and Elizabeth French.

Eliza said her brother Bill Dowell, who had been frying his supper over the fire, was almost too frightened to speak. He ate a little of his supper and then, within minutes, was round at Grapevine. People were gathering and entering the house. It seems the body of John Perryman had already been laid out. Dowell described

> a crowd outside and in. I spoke to James Minifie just inside of the door, and there were a great many in tears, and feeling mine coming I stepped outside for a minute or two until I regained my composure. ... Then I went in again and into the room where the deceased lay. I stayed there ten minutes and then went outside and said to the crowd, "Has any one gone for the doctor?" they said "yes." I said "Has any one gone for the policeman?" They said, "Yes, but we cannot find him." I said, "Which way have you been to look for him?" they said, "Down to his house." I said, "I will go up to the public house and look for him," as I knew he was very often there, but he was not there then. [5]

While Dowell hurried up the road to The Fountain Head, the village policeman, P. C. Martin, was on the far side of the village, coming back from Bovey, near Beer. William Ward and Mark Newton, who probably set off that way to find him, met him at about ten o'clock coming down Vicarage Hill. [6] They told him the news and all three went to Perryman's house, where they met Dowell returning with William Parrett from the pub.

Once P. C. Martin had arrived, a group of men, including Dowell, William Parrett and William Ward, accompanied him up the hill to examine the scene of the shooting and collect any of the dead man's possessions that were there. Many years later William Ward remembered the experience as frightening in the extreme because of the bright moonlight and the thought that the gunman could still be lurking nearby. [7] There is an old belief that men go mad at the full moon, and some people may have thought Perryman had been shot by a madman.

A dreadful rough path

After a while Martin and Dowell found themselves alone, the others having gone back down. As events unfold these two will became bitter antagonists, but standing here in the moonlight with blood on the grass,[8] they were still friends and collaborators. After some discussion, they decided to go together to visit Amos Power, the farmer who rented Culverwell Farm, which included Old Pits. Dowell, convinced the shooting was accidental, thought one of Amos Power's sons might have been out with a gun. Power lived at Elverway Farm in the northern valley, which meant they had to retrace Perryman's path through the pits (Figure 3, p.28). [9] Neither of them knew the way and it was by now, Dowell said, very dark; either the moon had set or it was hidden by clouds. Martin used his bullseye lantern, but they still had 'a fine old bother as it was a dreadful rough path and dangerous'. No doubt this part of their walk felt very scary. Things got easier when they reached Northern Lane, and they made their way down past Hole House to Hooknell.[10]

John Selway, the blacksmith who lived at Hooknell, said the only person he had seen out with a gun was Fred Skinner the gamekeeper, at about 8.50 p.m. on the moor near his house, about a mile from the shooting. [11] So they went on up the northern valley to Skinner's house at Beckham, and Skinner said, yes, he had been out shooting, but his last shot was at about seven o'clock, about half a mile from Old Pits. The two men, tired and thirsty, asked Skinner for some cider but he had none in the house.

Martin and Dowell must have decided that there was no point in continuing to Elverway, for they turned back home, stopping off at a place or two on the way. [12] Even so, it was three o'clock in the morning before they finally got back to Perryman's house. They were shown the old man's 'ruff bag' which had been brought down the hill, and his watch, indented by the shots. Apparently at

Dowell's suggestion, they checked out the bag for shot, found some, and then walked homewards down the road. After a final word on Dowell's doorstep, Martin trudged on down to his own house.

PART TWO
THE INQUEST OPENS, ARRESTS ARE MADE

CHAPTER FOUR

Rumour and the Press

Rumour

The news of the shooting flew around the village, followed very quickly by rumour and gossip. What had happened? Who had done it? Why? In any village, at any time, the rumour mill works overtime, and in Branscombe, as William Dowell put it: 'there was always some old tale about in the village with not a bit of truth in it'. But the shooting was an unprecedented occurrence and everyone would have been talking. On every doorstep, over every garden fence, in the pubs, out on the plats, and in the harvest fields, people would have picked over the details and debated the finest nuance of things said or seen. Important people in the village would have expressed their opinions publicly — whether farmers working alongside the harvesters, Reverend Swansborough pontificating from the pulpit, a Methodist preacher holding forth in the chapel, or Squire Ford riding round the parish — and they would have expected to be listened to.

Soon the gossip would have escaped the parish boundaries. Branscombe girls and women in service in surrounding towns, coming home on the Sunday after the shooting, heard what had happened and told the story on their return to work. Carriers and carters spread the word. Thirty-six hours after the event, when William Dowell's father took his cart to Sidmouth, rumours were already circulating there, and in the evening William Dowell complained bitterly to P. C. Martin 'My father has been to Sidmouth and someone told him that it was me that shot Perriman, and that I was run away'. [1]

Out of the welter of surmise, two stories began to emerge. The first, that Perryman had been accidentally shot by someone out poaching. The second, that it was an intentional killing but the assailant had shot the wrong man. A third story, that there had been a stranger in the village who had since disappeared, had more limited support. Opinions soon hardened, often along lines of social status, church or chapel, gender, and perhaps age. As the solicitor Every put it later: 'suspicion was rank', and friends, neighbours, even members of a family, might find themselves on opposite sides.

P. C. Martin, the local policeman, living amidst all this rumour and surmise, would have been influenced by it, but would also have tried to sift it for clues. But as the days went by, he might have found that people were less inclined to talk to him, that the bar fell silent when he entered. He was, after all, a relative outsider, and he represented the long and unloved arm of the law. Everyone in the village was related to everyone else, and however acrimonious the arguments became, no one would shop a relative, or give evidence that might result in a man being hanged. As *Pulman's Weekly News* noted, the police

> have had a difficult task to obtain the evidence now in hand, a great number of persons in the village being related or connected with the parties in the case. [2] (See Figure 5, p.80.)

The press

Local newspapers soon picked up the story. In normal circumstances Branscombe was unnewsworthy, more or less invisible, but once editors heard about the mysterious shooting they seized upon it. Curiously enough, it may have been William Dowell himself who, having penned a short account and sent it to the Yeovil-based *Pulman's Weekly News* on the Monday morning after the shooting, alerted them to what had happened. Certainly by Tuesday one or two reporters were in the village, sitting in on the first hearing of the inquest and filing detailed and almost verbatim accounts of the proceedings.

Two local papers especially, *Pulman's Weekly News* and *Trewman's Exeter Flying Post*, followed the story closely. The *Exeter Flying Post* came out a day after *Pulman's*, and their accounts are noticeably similar in tone and content, so it is possible, though unlikely, that one reporter was covering for both papers. The *Pulman's'* stories are somewhat more detailed, and we quote mainly from these. A third newspaper, *Lethaby's Sidmouth Journal,* came out only once a month, had a much smaller circulation, and could not afford a roving reporter. However, the editor, Richard Lethaby, followed the case with interest and though he was short on detail and came in on the tail of the others, he offered intelligent and trenchant commentaries.

The newspapers' detailed accounts have been a wonderful source for writing up the story of the shooting, and complement the pamphlet written by William Dowell. But newspapers are opinionated and take up certain positions at the expense of others. Then as now, there was an editorial bias in favour of the more sensational version. We have seen that at least two theories were circulating in the village — poaching accident or grudge-and-mistaken-identity — and the newspapers very quickly eliminated the first, less sensational, one.

The earliest report, which appeared in the *Exeter Flying Post* on the Wednesday, four days after the shooting, was written before the first findings had emerged at the inquest. It mainly described the death, but also offered a garbled version which confused the two theories:

> The person by whom the shot was fired was not discovered, and the cause of the outrage is unexplained. One theory is that the deceased was shot by poachers in mistake for another person against whom they had a grudge. [3]

Six days later, on Tuesday September 18, when *Pulman's Weekly News* filed its first long report, it detailed the evidence given at the first sitting of the inquest, separated out the two theories, and gave prominence to the more exciting grudge-and-mistaken-identity story. For, first, all agreed that Perryman was not the intended victim:

> the inhabitants are satisfied that no one intended to destroy the life of Perryman, who was looked upon by one and all as a "good old man".

Secondly, accidental shooting by a poacher was highly unlikely:

> Some persons look upon the affair as an accident in connection with a poaching expedition, but it is not probable that any man intending to illegally take game would have gone on a moonlight night with a gun to shoot on a path across a common well known to be frequented even at nine o'clock in the evening by labourers making their way from Mr Pyle's farm to their cottages down on the highway, only a gunshot below.

Therefore, thirdly, the grudge-and-mistaken-identity scenario was considered most likely:

> The rumour in which most faith is placed is that the person who fired the fatal shot premeditated and intended to murder an individual in Branscombe against whom there has been considerable ill-feeling fostered in consequence of a "neighbours quarrel".

And fourth, this was supported by the comment that, not only was the shot intended for someone else, but that a certain individual has left the neighbourhood since the occurrence. [4]

Richard Lethaby reported a similar balance of opinion:

> either that a poacher had in the dusk thought of firing at game, or that the injured man was mistaken for somebody else. The latter seemed to be the more prevalent opinion; indeed, there was again and again the whispered statement that So-and-So was the offender, and that such and such was the cause of the antipathy — threats having been muttered. [5]

The newspapers, therefore, all seemed to endorse the view that Perryman's death was a murder gone wrong. Lethaby's account, and also those given by the other papers, make it clear that some attempt was made to sound out village opinion, but it is likely that what they heard were the more vociferous opinions, those expressed in the pubs, or by influential members of the community.

On the other hand, the villagers would have been both impressed and influenced by the newspaper reports. Many were still illiterate, but there were always others ready to pore over the small print and read aloud to an attentive audience. Since the most usual reading matter in the village was the Bible, the printed word would have carried more authority than today. Newspaper versions of village gossip and the editorial bias they expressed would have fed back into village perceptions of what had happened on the fatal night, hardening and inflaming opinions.

CHAPTER FIVE

The Inquest Opens

At The Fountain Head inn

On September 11th, the Tuesday after the Saturday killing of John Perryman, Mr Charles Every Cox, Deputy Coroner, opened an inquest on his body at The Fountain Head inn. The duty of a Coroner's inquest is to establish the cause of death, not to discover a culprit or assign guilt — that is for the police and the criminal courts. In this instance the inquest and the criminal proceedings ran for a while in parallel, which complicated the Coroner's task but did not deflect him from it. A jury, apparently made up mainly of local farmers, was sworn in,[1] and the Coroner warned them that 'the affair which had called the jury together was of a very serious nature, and required a deal of investigation'. So it proved, for the inquest dragged on through three subsequent sessions and did not reach a verdict until a week into October.

Two village notables who were present for most of the time were Squire Henry Ford of Lower House and the Reverend Swansborough. John Pyle of Edge Farm, Perryman's employer, attended regularly. [2] Also present was Police Sergeant Jeffery from Honiton police station. *Pulman's Weekly News* noted that 'the greatest interest was manifested in the proceedings' and 'outside the public house a large number of villagers congregated for whom there was no room inside'. The Fountain Head is a small pub and was even smaller then, and it must have been a squeeze for the Coroner, jurymen, witnesses, reporters and a few privileged spectators to fit in between bar counter, front door and fireplace.

After initial formalities, the inquest heard a report from the police surgeon, Mr George Evans of Seaton. He had examined the body externally, found shot marks all over the chest, abdomen, face and head, but concluded that the principal part of the charge was between the upper part of the chest and the abdomen. In all probability death was caused from some internal injury. A *post mortem* examination would be necessary. (The Branscombe burial register shows that the body was buried by order of the Coroner the following day, for without refrigeration, *post mortems* had to be carried out very quickly.)

The Coroner then called as witnesses the labourers who returned from Edge Farm with Perryman, the men who had gone to his aid when he was shot, and the village constable who had examined the murder scene.

The witnesses

The first witness to be called was the last of the harvesters to have parted from Perryman, Robert Loveridge. He was born in Branscombe in 1840, the eldest of ten children of Emmanuel Loveridge, a labourer living at Sellers Wood in Branscombe but originally from Honiton. Aged 43, Robert Loveridge lived at Street with his wife and six children in a cottage owned by Henry Ford. Like Perryman, he rented a small cliff plat and worked as a farm labourer. [3]

He told the inquest that he had known Perryman for the past twenty years. They left Edge Farm at about twenty past eight on the evening of the 8th and walked down the road together. Perryman had 'said nothing to indicate that he was in fear of being attacked by anybody'. They climbed Culverwell Hill and 'were walking together on the hill previous to a quarter to nine o'clock, when they parted company'. Loveridge continued straight on over the hill to Street, and last saw Perryman at a quarter to nine, 'on the hill behind his house, walking in the direction of his home'. About 'five or seven minutes' later he heard the report of a gun, and although he 'thought it rather strange that a gun should have been fired at that time of night, he didn't think anything of a serious nature had happened' and went on home. [4] He heard no cries, and the moon was shining brightly. In later evidence he added that a person could be seen at 50 yards.

Thomas Newton, the next witness, aged 29, was born in Branscombe, the son of William Newton, also a labourer. Henry Ford's rent book for 1883 reveals that he had just moved to a cottage at Bridge with his wife, a lace-maker, and three daughters. [5] He too rented a small cliff plat. [6]

He told the inquest that he had walked down the road from Edge Farm with Perryman and Loveridge, and had last seen them at half past eight walking 'up the copse' — i.e. up through Hole Coppice. He heard no report of a gun, and only learned of Perryman's death 'after he had been home and partaken of his supper'.

The third witness, William Bartlett, aged 51, was born in Branscombe and lived at Blue Ball. [7] His wife and daughter were absent at the time of the 1881 census, but his wife was with him in 1891, his daughter having married in 1887. [8]

Blue Ball is near Grapevine and Bartlett was, as Thomas Newton said, 'in the habit of using the path on the hill where the deceased was shot'. Bartlett agreed that 'he generally accompanied the deceased on his way home, but he did not do so on Saturday evening' because he had 'stopped behind to pick up a few sticks for firewood'. But for this, commented a newspaper, 'in all probability he would have received part of the charge as well'. As it was, he heard no report of any firearms.

The last three labourers left Edge Farm too late to throw any new light on Perryman's movements, so the Coroner interrogated next the two young men who ran up the hill when they heard Perryman's cries for help. William Henry Tidwell was a labourer employed at Bulstone Farm and William James Williams was a baker employed at Bridge. [9] Tidwell told their story, and Williams corroborated it. They were walking together up through the village towards Street, and about 200 yards beyond Grapevine they heard Perryman's voice shouting 'Oh! Oh!' When Tidwell called out 'What's the matter?' the voice answered 'Come to me! Come to me!' Unable to see anything, they started up the side of Culverwell Hill, but when Tidwell called out again they heard only groans.

At this tense moment the inquest took a slightly comic turn. Tidwell said that when they reached Perryman he gasped out 'Someone has shot me; I heard the gun go off', which drew the following intervention and rebuke:

Mr Collins (a juryman): No, he said "I am shot".
Coroner: Silence, please. It is exceedingly wrong of you to interrupt a witness in that way.[10]

Collins's pedantry shows that the precise circumstances of Perryman's death had become a subject of detailed discussion in the village. Perhaps he thought the more neutral phrase 'I am shot' left open the possibility that the shooting was accidental rather than intentional. After the interruption Tidwell went on to say that when they lifted Perryman, blood 'fell from his mouth', and they called for help. It was about ten minutes before Thomas Ward arrived on the scene and helped them carry Perryman down, but 'he was dead when taken into his cottage'.

Finally, there was a brief statement from P. C. Martin. William Martin and his wife were Devon-born, but not natives of Branscombe, where he had been the village policeman for only three years. He was 31 and lived in Lower Church. He reported that no weapon had been found at the murder scene despite a wide search of the undergrowth. He produced Perryman's fob-watch, which was in a double case. An indentation on the back was 'caused apparently by a shot' and the 'key hanging to the chain was broken in two parts'. The watch had stopped at ten minutes to nine, corroborating Loveridge's estimate of when the shooting occurred.

The Coroner, concluding this first sitting of the inquest, remarked that it was 'scandalous that such an occurrence should have happened without the police being able to discover who the perpetrator of the deed was' but that 'perhaps the police had not had sufficient time to make full inquiries'. The jury were then bound over 'in their own recognizances of £10 each' and the inquest was adjourned for a fortnight.

CHAPTER SIX

Investigation, Arrest and Imprisonment

Nowadays, if a suspected murder occurs in a remote part of the country, the local police request outside help; the site of the shooting is sealed off, the area scoured, house-to-house inquiries are made, suspects are interrogated and alibis checked. In the late nineteenth century, such a flurry of activity seems to have occurred only if the victim belonged to the upper or professional classes. [1] But John Perryman was a poor man, and his assailant was likely to be a village nobody. Superintendent de Schmid, chief of the Honiton police division, which included Branscombe, seems to have felt no need to call in help, nor did he hurry to present himself in the village to take control of the situation. When the Coroner commented that perhaps the police had not had sufficient time to make full inquiries his voice may have held a tinge of sarcasm.

Investigation

As far as we can piece them together, the first five days of the police investigation went as follows:

Saturday 8 September: On the night of the shooting P. C. Martin visited the crime scene and walked across the parish with Dowell to see if anyone had been out with a gun. Martin was given Perryman's bag with some shot in it.

Sunday 9 September: Martin noted an impression in the brambles by the crime scene, and traced tracks leading away from it towards Upper Church. Dowell, Loveridge and others searched Culverwell Hill for a gun, in vain. Did Martin send a message to Honiton?

Monday 10 September: Martin probably went to Honiton and reported in person to Supt. de Schmid. By now Dowell must have been a suspect, because Martin went to Dunscombe to check out Dowell's statement that a gun he had sometimes used belonged to his brother-in-law, who had moved there and taken it with him. In the evening Martin went with Dowell to his sister's house, examined shot and powder flasks and removed some shot.

Tuesday 11 September: P. S. Jeffery came from Honiton. He and Martin attended the opening of the inquest at Branscombe.

Thursday 13 September: Supt. de Schmid came to Branscombe for the first time and ordered the constable to help in thoroughly searching the spot. He timed the walk between the site of the shooting and Dowell's house.

What stands out from this is that the crucial early stages of the investigation were left entirely to one village bobby, and to villagers such as Dowell who were willing to help him. How did Martin's mind work in those few days? On the Saturday night after the shooting, he had walked off trustingly into the darkness alone with Dowell. On Sunday evening Dowell, fancying himself as a freelance journalist, sought and received Martin's approval for a report on the shooting which he was about to send to *Pulman's Weekly News.* They 'then went down to the bottom of the village, and had several glasses of ale together' at The Masons Arms. [2] Dowell noticed nothing unusual in Martin's attitude, although Martin claimed later that he was already suspicious of Dowell but kept his thoughts to himself in order to draw him on. If Martin was telling the truth, what made him suspect Dowell by Sunday?

First, he had found the impression in the brambles at the crime scene. From there, a track seemed to lead in the direction of Upper Church, where Dowell lived. This would have suggested a possible link with a confrontation that he knew had happened at Upper Church a few days earlier, in which Amos French and David Pile had apparently quarrelled over Dowell's sister Eliza. And at some stage he must have learned that David Pile, against whom Eliza had a grievance, had been harvesting with Perryman at Edge Farm.

Linking these facts together might have convinced him that the Upper Church quarrel had led to an attempted murder which went wrong, and that the dominant opinion in the village, that the killing was not an accident but a case of mistaken identity, was correct.

But could his friend Dowell really be the murderer? He might have wanted to avenge an insult to his sister. He had held a license to shoot. Perhaps his keenness to help solve the mystery was camouflage, or an inability to stay away from the scene of his own crime? Against this, Martin knew Dowell well enough to realise that he was neither tough nor violent, and not at all a criminal type. Moreover, there were others who might have fled the crime scene in the direction of Upper Church, others who owned guns, and others more closely involved than Dowell in the recent quarrel.

Martin seems to have blocked out these other possibilities. It is not uncommon for the police to become fixated on one line of inquiry to the neglect of others, but Martin may also have been influenced by attacks on Dowell's character by people who disliked or envied him. Or possibly — and this is what Dowell came to suspect — he was summoned by the squire or the vicar to report on his findings, and encouraged — even, perhaps, given some inducement — to finger a man whom they regarded as an idler and a bad influence, a working man who spent his savings rather than work, and held radical political opinions.

Whatever persuaded him of Dowell's guilt, it seems probable that Martin took his half-baked theory to de Schmid on Monday, and that de Schmid was content to endorse it. Perhaps de Schmid told him to check the whereabouts of the gun Dowell had once used, and to search his house for powder and shot. In any case, the investigation now proceeded along this single track. De Schmid apparently thought he had done all that was necessary for the time being, and failed to put in an appearance at Branscombe until three days later, five days after the shooting.

Why was the Superintendent so lackadaisical? It is true that he had limited resources. The Honiton police establishment consisted only of himself, Police Sergeant William Jeffery, and three constables. He was also very inexperienced. [3] He was 35, but had only recently joined the police after ten years in the army, and presumably owed his appointment to being an officer and a gentleman rather than to any qualification for the job. This was almost certainly his first murder investigation.

Going through the newspaper reports we did wonder whether we might be applying twentieth-century standards to a nineteenth-century case, but were reassured to find that Richard Lethaby, in his Sidmouth paper, had no doubt at all about de Schmid's incompetence. Here, in a cutting dated 1 October 1883, Lethaby clearly believes, as we do, that class bias was implicit in this delay, and argued that the idea that it might be

> difficult to track the culprit, is preposterous; for there, unlike in Irish villages, assassins are not reared or sheltered, whilst the owners or users of guns must necessarily be few. Prompt action, and but a moderate share of that valuable faculty called "*nous*," would within a few hours have searched every nook and cranny, and every suspicious house and cottage. As it was, every day or hour which passed without discovery only tended to weaken the evidence for conviction, and remove the traces which shot, gun, movements, &c., would have furnished; and was not creditable to a highly-trained and numerous Police force, such as that which Devon possesses, with a Superintendent in residence at Honiton. Can it be that if instead of this unfortunate labourer being the victim, somebody of higher rank had fallen, there would have been more zeal and success? Suppose, for instance, the neighbour or gamekeeper of the late Lord of Wiscombe, C. Gordon, Esq., had been thus foully sent out of the world, can anybody hereabout doubt that within 48 hours he would have tracked the culprit? Aye, that he would.

HERBERT DE SCHMID – LOCAL POLICE CHIEF

Herbert William Ferdinand de Schmid was born in Florence in 1847, the son of a Prussian baron, Louis de Schmid, Chamberlain to the Duke of Parma. His mother Eliza was English; her father William Spence F. R. S. wrote a standard work on insects. With the creation of the Italian state in 1861, the dukedom of Parma disappeared; the Baron died in 1864, and his widow and sons moved to Springfield House, Ashprington, near Totnes, which she had inherited.

Herbert William tried his hand at business in London, and became a naturalized British subject in 1869. He joined the 2nd battalion of the Devon Militia in 1873, gazetted Captain in 1874. The regiment went to India and was ordered to march north to Kandahar in Afghanistan in 1880, where conditions were worse even than today. When Gladstone's new Liberal government reversed Disraeli's forward policy in Afghanistan, the 2nd Devons were ordered back to India, and reached the Punjab in 1881 with the loss of half their officers and men from dysentery.[4] Captain de Schmid purchased his discharge from the army in 1882, and was Superintendent of Police at Honiton by December that year.

RICHARD LETHABY—LOCAL LIBERAL CONSCIENCE

Lethaby's editorials were the only articles that went beyond the details of the Perryman case to wider issues. Born in Chulmleigh, Devon, in 1812. He was manager for a well-known military publisher in London, Messrs Clowes & Sons, but came back to Devon in 1861. He took over a printing & publishing business in the Market Place, Sidmouth and edited and published *Lethaby's Sidmouth Journal* until shortly before his death in 1888. He was a Methodist, a Liberal, a temperance campaigner and a member of the R.S.P.C.A. [5]

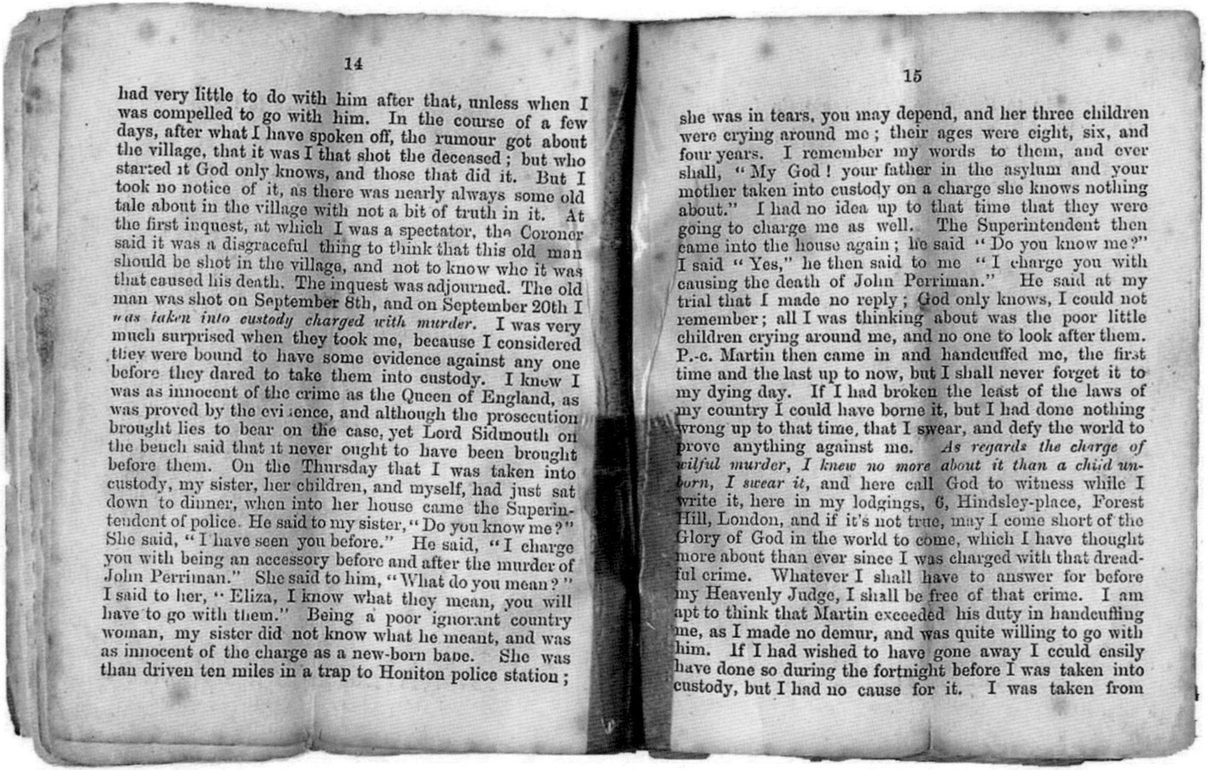

14

had very little to do with him after that, unless when I was compelled to go with him. In the course of a few days, after what I have spoken off, the rumour got about the village, that it was I that shot the deceased; but who started it God only knows, and those that did it. But I took no notice of it, as there was nearly always some old tale about in the village with not a bit of truth in it. At the first inquest, at which I was a spectator, the Coroner said it was a disgraceful thing to think that this old man should be shot in the village, and not to know who it was that caused his death. The inquest was adjourned. The old man was shot on September 8th, and on September 20th I *was taken into custody charged with murder.* I was very much surprised when they took me, because I considered they were bound to have some evidence against any one before they dared to take them into custody. I knew I was as innocent of the crime as the Queen of England, as was proved by the evidence, and although the prosecution brought lies to bear on the case, yet Lord Sidmouth on the bench said that it never ought to have been brought before them. On the Thursday that I was taken into custody, my sister, her children, and myself, had just sat down to dinner, when into her house came the Superintendent of police. He said to my sister, "Do you know me?" She said, "I have seen you before." He said, "I charge you with being an accessory before and after the murder of John Perriman." She said to him, "What do you mean?" I said to her, "Eliza, I know what they mean, you will have to go with them." Being a poor ignorant country woman, my sister did not know what he meant, and was as innocent of the charge as a new-born babe. She was than driven ten miles in a trap to Honiton police station;

15

she was in tears, you may depend, and her three children were crying around me; their ages were eight, six, and four years. I remember my words to them, and ever shall, "My God! your father in the asylum and your mother taken into custody on a charge she knows nothing about." I had no idea up to that time that they were going to charge me as well. The Superintendent then came into the house again; he said "Do you know me?" I said "Yes," he then said to me "I charge you with causing the death of John Perriman." He said at my trial that I made no reply; God only knows, I could not remember; all I was thinking about was the poor little children crying around me, and no one to look after them. P.-c. Martin then came in and handcuffed me, the first time and the last up to now, but I shall never forget it to my dying day. If I had broken the least of the laws of my country I could have borne it, but I had done nothing wrong up to that time, that I swear, and defy the world to prove anything against me. *As regards the charge of wilful murder, I knew no more about it than a child unborn, I swear it,* and here call God to witness while I write it, here in my lodgings, 6, Hindsley-place, Forest Hill, London, and if it's not true, may I come short of the Glory of God in the world to come, which I have thought more about than ever since I was charged with that dreadful crime. Whatever I shall have to answer for before my Heavenly Judge, I shall be free of that crime. I am apt to think that Martin exceeded his duty in handcuffing me, as I made no demur, and was quite willing to go with him. If I had wished to have gone away I could easily have done so during the fortnight before I was taken into custody, but I had no cause for it. I was taken from

Figure 4: William Dean Dowell's account of his arrest

The arrest

Twelve days after the shooting, on Thursday 20th September, Superintendent de Schmid, P. S. Jeffery and P. C. Richard Slee descended on Branscombe, where P. C. Martin joined them. De Schmid walked into Eliza Williams's house at Upper Church where she, her brother and the children were having dinner. Then, as Bill Dowell recounted:

> He said to my sister, "Do you know me?" She said, "I have seen you before." He said, "I charge you with being an accessory before and after the murder of John Perryman." She said to him, "What do you mean?" I said to her, "Eliza, I know what they mean, you will have to go with them." Being a poor ignorant country woman, my sister did not know what he meant, and was as innocent of the charge as a new-born babe.
>
> She was in tears, you may depend, and her three children were crying around me; their ages were eight, six and four years ... I had no idea up to that time that they were going to charge me as well.

P. S. Jeffery escorted Eliza to Honiton in a pony trap, and de Schmid returned to Dowell in the house:

> He said, "Do you know me?" I said "Yes," he then said to me "I charge you with causing the death of John Perriman." [6]

At Honiton police court the next day de Schmid said that the arrest occurred at 1.30 p.m. and that the accused was then handed over to P. C. Martin who took him to Honiton. Here is Dowell again:

> P.-c. Martin then came in and handcuffed me, the first time and the last up to now, but I shall never forget it to my dying day. ... I was taken from Branscombe to Seaton to catch the train for Honiton (police cells), at which town I was tried.

> Before I left Branscombe P.-c. Martin, my bosom friend as I thought, took me in a public house while he sent for a conveyance to take me to Seaton station. While I was there John Croom asked me to drink out of his pint, but P.-c. Martin wouldn't allow me, although he took me here. Mrs Clarke, the Landlady, saw I was very much upset, and she gave me a drop of brandy but Martin wouldn't allow me to drink it. [7]

Meanwhile Eliza's neighbour Amos French had also been arrested as an accessory. He too was taken to The Masons Arms before being sent on to Honiton, but was treated more kindly:

> A strange policeman [P. C. Slee] took French … he never handcuffed him, and he took him to the same public-house and payed for some drink for him.

In the cells

Once at Honiton police station, the three suspects were searched and put in the cells. The only account we have for this part of the story is Bill Dowell's, and it is very graphic. The three cells were in a line, Amos was placed in the first one, Eliza in the second, and Bill in the third — 'the condemned cell I suppose'. He wrote:

> I shall never forget my feelings when the door of the cell closed against me with its double lock, I thought my heart would have ceased beating, a dreadful sensation passed over me. [8]

After a while he calmed down. Surely, now they had been arrested, the guilty person would come forward? He went to a hole in the door and spoke to his sister and Amos. They talked then, and for the rest of the week, about the 'cruel way in which [they] had been served'. They did not realise that the police were listening to every word they said, although, as Bill comments, they did not get 'a tittle of evidence against us'. But knowing he was not guilty did not dispel the thought that many an innocent man had hung.

Eliza had a Bible in her cell, and

> ... she asked us if she should read a chapter to us. We said yes, we could hear from the little cell windows. She told me that she took the bible and let it open where it would, and read the first chapter that came to her view, and it was the 35th Psalm. If she had looked the bible through she could not have found a chapter more suitable to our own case. She read that chapter to us dozens of times during the week we were there. It is where David prayeth for his own safety and his enemies' confusion, and of their wrongful dealings with him; and God knows we had cause for it as much as David. [9]

It is easy to see why the psalm meant so much to them, and why they asked her to read it so many times:

> Plead my cause, O Lord, with them that strive with me: fight against them that fight against me. ...
> False witnesses did rise up; they laid to my charge things that I knew not. ...
> Let not them that are mine enemies wrongfully rejoice over me: neither let them wink with the eye that hate me without a cause ...
> Let them be ashamed and brought to confusion together that rejoice at mine hurt: let them be clothed with shame and dishonour that magnify themselves against me.

This passage of holy writ, so miraculously revealed, may have strengthened Dowell's belief that they were the victims of a whispering campaign, and had been deliberately framed.

The next day, after a sleepless night on bare boards, they were brought before the magistrates. The newspaper reported that 'All three prisoners wore a very anxious appearance' [10] and that Dowell's eyes appeared red. [11] Because de Schmid was granted first one, and then another adjournment, they had to spend nearly a week in the cells. During this time P. C. Slee was mostly in charge, and eighteen months later Bill Dowell wrote, having been told that 'this poor fellow has died since then', that 'I was very sorry to hear it as he treated us with every respect while in the cells'. [12]

When first taken into custody, Bill was so sure of his innocence that he declared he would not 'spend a farthing over the case'. But by Monday he and the others began to realise that, innocent or not, they had better pay someone to defend them. Sergeant Jeffery tried to dissuade them, which Bill found rather strange.[13] Nevertheless they engaged Mr William Every, a Honiton solicitor, and Bill ended up paying him £25 plus expenses. [14] He bemoaned the fact that having 'employed counsel ... it closed my mouth', which explains why he found himself frequently interrupting the proceedings! But since they were in effect tried twice, by the magistrates in Honiton and by the Coroner in Branscombe, they had much need of Every's services, and he did well by them.

We pause now to get to know the three suspects better, especially Bill Dowell, the central figure in our story, before looking more closely at why the police picked on them as culprits.

PART THREE
THE ACCUSED

CHAPTER SEVEN

The Accused Murderer

Dowell's pamphlet *The Life of William Dean Dowell, the Accused Murderer*, was published in London in 1885. In it he told his life-story and tried to set his experiences in Branscombe in a larger social and political context. It is a piece of passionate pleading and a political tract as well as a narrative, and the thoughts and feelings he expresses so freely tell us a great deal about him, as does the mere fact that he, a working man, wrote and published it. Close reading of the press coverage of the case also reveals much about his personality and conduct, both in day-to-day village life before his arrest and in the tense atmosphere of court hearings. In this chapter we try to see what sort of a man he was, what figure he cut in Branscombe, and how the years spent making a living in big cities had given him attitudes and political views sharply at odds with those of a conservative, squire-dominated rural backwater.

Early years

William Dean Dowell, Bill Dowell as everyone called him, was born in 1852, the son of John Tucker Dowell (1825-1919). There had been Dowells in Branscombe since the early eighteenth century. His great-grandfather Amos (1775-1865) was a thatcher, and two of Amos's sons, John and Tobias, had followed him in the trade. Amos, John and Tobias lived at Vicarage and in 1850 all three were members of the church choir. Amos's third son, James, William's grandfather, became a tailor and moved to Street. Village tailors did not earn much, and his eldest son John Tucker Dowell began life as a shepherd and farm labourer. When he married Amelia Dean (1828-1914) in 1848, they set up home at New Linhay, a tied cottage near Edge Farm which is still recognisable despite later extension and ruination.

William was born at New Linhay, the third of ten children and the eldest of three or possibly four boys. At least one of the children died in infancy. Here is Dowell's own account of his early years:

> I was born in the County of Devon, east, parish of Branscombe, in the year 1852 … I was born of poor, but respectable, parents, my father at that time being a farm labourer whose wages were from 7s. to 8s. per week ... Until I was nine years of age I had but very little schooling. At nine I went out to work driving the plough oxen,[1] and lived in two farm houses; my wages were from 6d. to 1s. per week. That brings me to the age of 14.

Consider the implications. The family was so poor that Bill, aged nine, was already working full-time and living away from home. He also tells us that he often went hungry to bed and that, although he grew up to be a church-goer, the only schooling he had was at the Wesleyan Sunday school, where his teacher was John Perryman, the man he was accused of killing.

Gradually life improved. By the time Bill reached fourteen, his father had gone up a bit in the world, and had

> through his own industry, raised himself from being a farm labourer to be the owner of a horse and cart, going about dealing in pigs, poultry, cheese etc. … After he had improved his position he thought he would like to put me to a trade, and bring me out of the bonds of slavery ... I said I would like to be a carpenter; he got me a place at Sidmouth, six miles from Branscombe, with Richard Tucker, builder, with whom I was bound apprentice for five years, from 1867 until 1872. … When my time was out my master gave me 10s. and my mistress a new bible, which I have now. [2]

Bill's time in Sidmouth came to an end in 1873, and he worked for a short while in Exeter before moving to South Wales, like many other Devon men in this period of coal-based industrial development.

Alone in the gallery

Dowell recounted only one village event from his Sidmouth years. No doubt he told this story to show that even at a young age he was capable of acting independently and flouting village authority. He may also have thought that his youthful behaviour affected village attitudes to him when Perryman was killed.

The event, set in 1871, involves the Reverend Henry George Tomkins, whose eulogy of John Perryman was quoted in Chapter 2. Dowell himself thought that Tomkins was

> the best Vicar the parish ever had, as he studied the welfare of the poor, both the chapel-goers and the church alike, and gave them many a good meal when they would have had none. [3]

But Tomkins's ministry lasted only four years, from 1868 to 1872, for by 1871 he was locked in conflict with Henry Ford, and was eventually forced to resign. [4]

The story goes like this: before Tomkins's arrival, the Ford family had got used to running the church. The Reverend Peppin had grown old and infirm and raised no objection when Henry Ford took over Vestry meetings, or when his spinster aunt Mary Ford installed a harmonium in the church gallery and appointed herself organist, and his bachelor uncle William Braddick Ford, also installed in the gallery, ran the choir. These two old folk had their own views about church music, and Tomkins, when he arrived, had his. A clash was inevitable, and came in 1870 at a special service held to launch the fund for the new village school, at which the Archdeacon came to preach.

The service went badly wrong: the organ sounded off when it should not have, and both organ and choir refused to make any sound at all when they should have. This was probably due to confusion, but Tomkins attributed the discordant noise made by Miss Ford to a disposition on her part to annoy him. He promptly sacked both organist and choir, and banned the two elderly Fords from the gallery.

From this *contretemps* a bitter feud developed. The Fords and their cronies boycotted the church, and Dowell, while apprenticed in Sidmouth, witnessed the result:

> The Fords fell out with him and kept away from church, and of course all the tenants of the Fords. When I used to go home from Sidmouth to Branscombe I used to go to church just the same. Being a member of Sidmouth church and schools, I have been down to church after the fall out, perhaps there were no more than seven or eight people there, the choir had all left. The vicar, Mr Thomkins (*sic*), would give out the hymns and start the tune, and I, in the gallery, would join in, and there might be a woman in the body of the church squeak in, and so they got on for some time . . . [5]

Encouraged by the Archdeacon, Tomkins prosecuted William Braddick Ford and Mary Ford at Honiton petty sessions for disturbing divine service, but Lord Sidmouth threw the case out, remarking that if a little concession had been made on each side, it need never have been brought before them. Tomkins proceeded to air his complaints in the local press, whereupon Henry Ford arranged a presentation dinner for his aunt at The Masons Arms, William Braddick Ford gave a ball for the farmers, and Mary Ford distributed Christmas gifts to the poor to curry favour in the village.

In 1871 Tomkins challenged a rota by which the village ratepayers, mostly farmers, took turns to fill the two posts of churchwarden, and when he took the issue to the Archdeacon's court, he won. But soon, according to Dowell,

> ... they drove him from the village after all, in this way: — One 5th of November they dressed up a guy to represent the vicar, with surplice on and bible in hand and paraded him through the village and then burnt his effigy in front of his house, surplice, bible and all. I believe that these proceedings nearly broke him down.

Dowell is our only source for this unruly event, but he can be trusted because there were a number of other such cases. It is not clear who 'they' were, although Dowell had no doubt about it:

> I can sympathise with him as I have been served the same as he was, through acting the noble part, but much worse and by the same class of people. The farmers would do anything if they thought it would please their landlord, not because their farms are cheap as they pay high rents, but because they don't know any better. [6]

And as we shall see, Dowell was indeed served the same way. Tomkins himself left the village soon after, gave up parish work and devoted himself to biblical scholarship.

The making of a radical

The spark of independence which kept young Bill Dowell in the boycotted church on Sundays was fanned into a flame of political radicalism by his experience of working-class solidarity and the political reform movements of the early 1880s.

In Wales he had worked for Thomas Williams, a Cardiff builder. The mid-Victorian boom in church-building was still in full swing in the early 'seventies, and his first job was at Llanfrechfa Church, Monmouthshire, no doubt on the hefty rafters which still support its roof. Then he was employed on a new church in Llanelly, Carmarthenshire, where he stayed a few years, educated himself at Sunday school, saved money, and opened his first Post Office savings account. Why did he particularly tell us this?

> I state this because a big bug in Branscombe dared to ask a companion of mine where I got my money from. I will tell

> him to his face one day — by the sweat of my brow, 57 hours per week. Not the same way that he got his: by telling a cock-and-bull story two hours per week. [7]

The big bug who works only two hours a week must be the Reverend Swansborough, Tomkins's successor, whom Dowell found to be not at all the warm-hearted vicar described by newspapers, but part of an oppressive Tory establishment. Here, under the guise of curiosity, Swansborough came close to encouraging the malicious gossip about Dowell that divided the village.

After Llanelly, Dowell had moved to Pembroke Dock, then through the Midlands to Manchester. But 'as a great strike broke out there amongst the carpenters and joiners, and as I belonged to the Trade Society I did not dare to work there'. His trade society was the Amalgamated Society of Carpenters and Joiners, formed in London in 1860. It became one of the largest and most important trade unions of the Victorian era under its moderate leader Robert Applegarth, general secretary from 1862 to 1871, who was a Liberal. But in 1877 the union got embroiled in a disastrous twelve-month strike in Manchester, and Dowell was wise to move on.

He went to Birmingham, lodged at 36 Aston Road, and over the next two or three years he started to attend political meetings:

> I had the honour of listening to three of England's greatest and best men. My views up to that time had been Conservative, but after listening to Gladstone, Bright and Chamberlain on the oppression of the poor I knew what they said was true, for I had witnessed it in my own native village. Theirs is the Party that will do good for the oppressed labourers ... [8]

Dowell was fortunate to hear these orators at the height of their powers, and before the Liberal Party split over Irish Home Rule in 1886, which divided Chamberlain and Bright from Gladstone. Before that, all three were united in wanting to give rural workers the vote, and when Dowell set their promises against the blatant inequality and wage-slavery in his beloved Branscombe — 'the village I called home, and the home of my forefathers for generations' [9] — it is no wonder he responded to their new democratic message. On occasional visits home he began to talk politics:

> I dared to say a few words ... in my native village, where they are all Tories, so I was rather looked down on, but that is no reason why they should try to hang me for it. [10]

In 1880 Dowell came south to join his two younger brothers in London. They had followed his example by seeking a living in the wider world, and the 1881 census shows Fred Dowell (24) living at 7 Hindsley Place, Forest Hill, Lewisham, with his wife, a Londoner, and their baby daughter. His younger brother Lewis (16) was living with him. Both young men were fishmongers, and Fred had probably already established the fish shop in Perry Vale which they were still managing together twenty years later. Bill Dowell took lodgings next door in Hindsley Place, and then, at Christmas 1881, 'trade being rather dull', came home to Branscombe, with money in his pocket, to enjoy himself. He intended to return to London in the Spring of 1882, but became 'dangerously ill'. His trade union provided sick pay of 12s a week, but when these payments ceased he was still unwell. In August 1883 he again decided to leave the village, but hearing that trade was still bad, he — unfortunately — stayed on.

The return of the native

Dowell was nothing like Clym Yeobright in Thomas Hardy's *The Return of the Native* but he was in a somewhat similar position, a returned native who no longer fitted in. He had changed a lot while the village had changed much less, and one can feel the tension.

Once he had been fingered as a murderer, it was easy for the villagers to see everything about him as dubious and suspicious, just because he was a bit different. For example, because he was staying with his sister Eliza, who lived at Upper Church with her three children, a reporter, retailing village gossip, wrote

> he returned to Branscombe, stating that he came home through ill health. Since then he has lived with his sister, but he hasn't followed any occupation ... His father and mother reside in Branscombe but he didn't live with them as there had been a dispute. [11]

Not so, says Dowell:

> The reason I lived with my sister was that I was at home when her husband was taken to the Asylum [in 1879]. She came to my father's house, and asked me to come to her and stop, as she was timid. I did so, and when I have gone home since, I have always made that my home.[12]

He was in a no-win situation: whatever he did was liable to be misconstrued. Another example: he was generous with his money, and in 1878, when his mother wrote to him about poverty in the village, he offered to send 10s, or £1 to any family in need, and on his return:

> If there was anyone in trouble in the village and I knew it, I was always the first to go to their assistance with advice and money, and there are people lying in Branscombe churchyard to-day, if they could speak they would thank Bill Dowell for what he had done. ... I remember the case of Jack Farrant and Lewis Perryman, two lads of Branscombe that got in a little trouble, whom I tried to keep from a felon's cell … with money and advice.[13]

The recipients would have been grateful, no doubt, but others might feel he was getting too big for his boots. Dowell found that he was criticised when he took out a licence to shoot (even though he did not have a gun) and when he acquired a fox terrier— 'That's a dreadful crime in these villages, where landlordism, tyranny, and oppression is rampant'. [14] Ordinary folk could not afford pets, and not only the privileged owners of gun-dogs and sheepdogs, but also some of his fellow villagers may well have disapproved.

Those who knew him well described him as friendly, good-humoured and gentle. Isaac French, the village carrier, who spent a great deal of time propping up the bar at The Black Lion inn in

Honiton, called him 'a quiet little man'. His sister Eliza said she had 'never heard him speak disrespectfully against anyone in my life'. He was on good terms with his neighbours: Sarah Anne Northcott said she had never seen him out of temper, and he was 'good friends' with David Pile — 'about a week before [the shooting] he gave me some cabbage out of his garden and I gave him 4d. for it', said Dowell. He was easy with Amos French, who, finding him in his house with his wife and daughter when he came home, greeted him with 'Well old man, how be 'ee getting on?' [15]

He was also gregarious and spent a fair amount of time in the pub, mainly The Fountain Head. Late on Saturday afternoon before the shooting Eliza had to persuade him to leave the bar and come home to tea; on Sunday he walked down to The Masons Arms for a pint with P. C. Martin; and on Monday evening Martin met him coming out of The Fountain Head with some companions. He also had a personal reason for frequenting this particular pub, for his girl-friend was Susan Ann Gill, the sister of the landlord, Thomas Gill. He had left The Masons Arms on Sunday night 'as I had to go and see my girl'. And next day, 'Miss Gill had been with him' when he walked down with Martin from The Fountain Head to Eliza's house. [16] In general, he was clubbable with men, but liked the company of women. He gossiped with Mrs Northcott and asked young Bessie Raffell whether he might walk her down the road.

So, on the one hand, Bill Dowell was seemingly well liked. He wrote: 'When I went home they were always glad to see me as I was not like some that went away from the village and came home and would not speak to them'. On the other hand, the distance was there. There is something a little patronising in the way he wrote 'I was always proud to shake the hand of such class of men as I have mentioned, and felt for them in their oppression, as they work very hard for the enormous sum of 10s. per week', and in his description of his sister as 'a poor ignorant country woman'. [17]

No doubt he flaunted his literacy. Many people in the village could read and write a little, and many households read one of the weekly newspapers, but no one else, even if they could write a letter, would have thought of writing a report for the local paper, as

Dowell did.[18] No one else would have considered writing and publishing an autobiographical pamphlet, nor felt, as Dowell did, that the eye of the world was upon him. 'My character', he said, after the verdict, 'has been vilified, and it had gone throughout the world. I wish the Press to take notice of the decision today'.[19]

Fred Dowell

So he was a man who no longer quite fitted in. The only physical descriptions we have of him are Isaac French's alleged reference to him as a 'little man', and a reporter's sketch: 'He is of dark complexion, wears a black moustache, and is well dressed'.[20] Perhaps he looked rather like his brother Fred (alongside).

We know he took things hard. We are told, more than once, that during the proceedings he was emotional and easily agitated. Dowell cried after the verdict was given, and a little later burst out: 'I never was so hurt in my life. I never thought of such a thing. It is more than a man can bear'.[21] He acknowledged that he was 'a very feeling and sensitive chap', and described with horror what it felt like to be incarcerated:

> I went to the wooden bed and kneeling down, shed a few tears, the first time for many years, but since then I have shed thousands over this cruel case. I am the wreck of a man through it to-day; the reason I feel it so much is that I had never thought to injure a soul in my whole life, by word or deed, neither had I done so.[22]

'Them that are mine enemies'

Again and again in his pamphlet Dowell bursts out in angry self-pity. His certainty that his arrest was due to the machinations of enemies sounds almost paranoid, though it may not have been entirely unfounded. So who did he think they were, these 'false witnesses' who 'hate me without a cause', as the psalmist put it?

Foremost amongst his targets was P. C. Martin, whom he blamed for betraying his trust. Perhaps because he was half-aware of the distance that had grown up between himself and the villagers, Dowell had turned to Martin for friendship. Already, in London, he had found that policemen were a betwixt-and-between class of men with whom he felt comfortable:

> nearly all my companions in Forest Hill were in the Metropolitan police force, and I have been with them many times when they were on special duty, and I always found them upright and just in doing their duty both to rich and poor alike. ... When I got home I treated this Devon county policeman with the same respect ... [23]

Consequently,

> I was about with P.-c. Martin more than I was with any man in the village. I have been scores of miles with him, played hundreds of game of shove-halfpenny, all one night at cards, when no doubt he ought to have been on duty, and about a fortnight before the murder he sent his child to my house asking me to go out to Southleigh with him as he had a job on there. ... He asked me to go with him to the "Three Horse Shoes" public-house in Colyton parish where I paid for four quarts of 6d. ale for him and myself and Keeper Skinner, who was with us ... [24]

But it turned out that in Martin he was 'sheltering a venemous [*sic*] serpent in [his] breast', and dismay and bitterness at this betrayal colours his account. We show in a later chapter how he tried to refute Martin's testimony against him point by point, accusing him of perjury and lies. 'No doubt if he had got me hung he would have gained a stripe through it, and perhaps £100 in the bargain ... I cannot say he was offered money to do it, but it looks to me very much like it.' [25] Thinking back on their pub jaunts, he added: 'he knew I was a good-tempered fool, and spent my money on him and others in the village foolishly'. Sure of his own innocence, it never occurred to him to wonder if Martin might have acted out of a mistaken sense of duty. But then, it is almost as hard for us as it was for Dowell to believe that Martin could have found the evidence compelling, and was not put up to it by someone.

Dowell knew he had enemies among the villagers, and singled out a family related to a wizard whom he had accused of exploiting their credulity:

> When I got home, in 1881, my sister told me she had paid a man a sovereign to go and see her husband in Exminster Asylum, as the people had made her believe that her husband was bewitched; and this old wizard, or wise man, Cross, of Newton Abbott, went to the asylum and saw him, and told her she was to do the most ridiculous nonsense I ever heard of. When she told me of it I was very angry, and wrote off at once to this Cross, of Newton Abbott, threatening him with proceedings in the police court if he did not refund the money which my sister had paid him. He did so, but I ought to have summoned him for getting money under false pretences. He gets many pounds from the ignorant of that village, so I got disliked by his worshippers instead of thanked for it. When I was taken ill it was because I got the money back from Cross; all my troubles they trace to that, even the murder case. [26]

Just as Dowell's scepticism about magic put up some village backs, so his political radicalism made him unpopular with Conservatives. Farmers would have seen him as setting a noxious example by enjoying the benefits of trade union membership, such as sick pay. Among Henry Ford's papers in the Devon Record Office is *Pulman's Weekly News* for 20 August 1872, marked 'Do not destroy'. Under the headline 'The Agricultural Labourers' Question' it reports a meeting of a thousand or so farm-workers and their families at Ilminster. Joseph Arch, founder of the short-lived National Agricultural Workers Union, told them that unionization was the only remedy for their wrongs — for having to pay 2s or 2s 6d a week rent out of a weekly wage of 9s, for being unpaid if they missed a day's work, and for having to work overtime for nothing but 'a little washgut cider'. George Potter, the firebrand editor of the trade union journal *The Beehive,* was applauded for saying that 'the country was made up of two classes — one class having more dinners than appetites, and the other having more appetites than dinners to consume'. But so far the trade union movement had made little headway in rural Devon, and landlords and farmers were determined to keep it that way.

Dowell himself thought he was framed for political reasons, because, as he said, he had 'dared to speak a word in defence of the poor oppressed labourers of my native village'. [27] His prosecution was certainly the result of a shambolic police investigation, but was it also politically motivated? We shall return to this question later.

Before Dowell left the village he finally asked Martin why he had been arrested, and 'he said to me I must thank my friends that ever I was charged with murder'. Who did he mean? No one gave evidence against him. Martin sounds close to admitting that he was swayed by hostile opinion in the village, but whose? Dowell's immediate response to Martin's cryptic comment was: 'the rich of Branscombe were not my friends, quite the reverse'. [28] Was this what Martin meant? Dowell also said 'I know that I had three or four powerful enemies in the village, and I will name them if ever this case is found out, and why they went against me' — but the case never was found out and he never named them.

A broken man

Before his arrest and trial Bill Dowell felt he had made something of himself, understood the ways of world, and could open the eyes and minds of his fellow villagers. But this ordeal turned everything upside down — he felt that his best chum had betrayed him, villagers had turned against him, and powerful enemies had almost succeeded in getting rid of him altogether. His world had crumbled and could not easily be put together again. His life, he said, had been ruined, 'in every shape and form':

On the day before I was taken into custody I was singing the song entitled "Justice in England". Little did I think then I was going to suffer next day and ever after through the injustice of England. I often think of it, but have never sung since. [29]

CHAPTER EIGHT

The Accomplices

Eliza Williams, Bill Dowell's elder sister, and Amos French, their neighbour, were charged as accessories before and after the fact, implying that they knew Dowell intended to kill Perryman, perhaps encouraged or conspired with him, and protected him afterwards. What do we know about these two people?

Eliza Williams

Eliza was the firstborn child of John and Amelia Dowell — she was born only four months after their marriage in January 1848. The family's poverty lasted throughout her childhood, and it must have been hard to be both the oldest and a girl. She had very little schooling but she learnt to read, probably, like Bill, at John Perryman's Sunday school. In the census of 1861 she was thirteen and already described as a lace-maker.

In 1874, aged twenty-six, she married Thomas Williams, who was a year younger than herself and came from a remarkable but ill-starred family. His father, Matthew Williams (also known as Westbye) was born in 1796 or 1798 in Denmark. We have not been able to discover why or how he fetched up in Branscombe,[1] but in 1820 he married Sarah French. Four sons were born between 1824 and 1841, John, William, Matthew, and George; George died aged six. Thomas — Eliza's husband-to-be — was not born until 1849, about a year after George's death, but unlike the others he was not christened. Sarah was forty-nine by this time, very old for child-bearing, and it is possible that Thomas was the illegitimate son of her sixteen-year old daughter Susan.

Matthew Williams senior was an enterprising man. Described variously in censuses as labourer, cordwainer (shoemaker), beer retailer and cliff farmer, he was, more importantly, a successful smuggler. John Gill, who was involved in smuggling as a young boy, gave this account to the antiquarian J. Y. A. Morshead: [2]

> All the smuggled spirits old farmer Williams imported used to be brought to [my fathers house] and my father diluted them, sometimes they went off undiluted in wagons or in tin cases that fitted men's pockets. Williams' goods came in French luggers — I don't know from what port — Rattenbury was more respected for he ran his own goods mostly. [3]

We are also told that Williams and Bray (a smuggler who farmed at Woodhead) probably footed the bill when an effigy of the turnpike keeper at Trow, who had informed against Bray, was paraded through Sidbury, Salcombe and Branscombe and then burnt. [4]

Matthew Williams invested his illicit earnings in property. First, in 1830, he secured a copyhold tenure of two cottages at Upper Church (now part of Coombe House); then he built two more houses (now Country House and Country Cottage) on the adjacent land. Country House has a capacious barrel-vaulted room dug into the hillside with a light-well, or trapdoor access, in the roof. Maybe it was once a storeroom for contraband, screened from the front room by a false wall. Much of the present story revolves around these houses.

Matthew was not only a smuggler and a man of property but also a regular church-goer. He and his two sons, John and Matthew, sang in the church choir. [5] Night-time games of cat-and-mouse with coastguards sat quite easily alongside Sunday pieties. On the other hand, John Gill junior, when recounting his smuggling stories to Morshead, wondered whether the madness that affected the Williams family, as well as the Leighs of Weston, might have been the effect of a bad conscience about smuggling: 'Squire Leigh died mad and both young Williams are in the asylum now. Perhaps their consciences worked them, but mine doesn't' (see over).

Eliza was Thomas Williams's second wife. In 1869, aged twenty, he had married Mary Loving. They had a daughter, but in 1873 both Mary and her child died. A year later he married Eliza and they

THE WILLIAMS BOYS – PROSPERITY AND MADNESS

Of Matthew Williams's four sons, only the eldest, John (1824-1887), showed no sign of madness. He was a butcher and landlord of The Masons Arms. His daughter Lavinia recalled her mother hiding tubs of smuggled brandy under her skirts while an Excise Officer searched his pub. [6] As the freeholder of several cottages, John could vote in elections. [7]

The second son, William Roberts Williams (1826-1886), a tailor and cliff-farmer, was the village carrier before Isaac French. [8] He lived at Cliff View Cottage, near the church, and his father lived with him from 1874. He inherited Matthew's four houses at Upper Church and later bought the freeholds. But in 1886, for undiscovered reasons, he cut his throat. [9]

The third son, Matthew Williams, junior (1830-1906) was a labourer living at Street. He rented a cliff plat, and followed the family tradition of smuggling. In October 1861, given the choice of a £100 fine or 6 months in gaol, he chose the latter. He wrote a long poem about his arrest and imprisonment, which was framed and passed down in his family. [10]

Soon after his release in 1862, and again in 1875, he became insane and was sent to Exminster Asylum. George Evans (the Seaton surgeon who was to perform the *post mortem* on John Perryman) described his 'delusions that he has a number of people who visit him in the night, and that he has fought with the devil'. His brother John vouched for 'threats that he would kill his wife'. He was released again, but his brother William's suicide in 1886 brought on 'a state of constant melancholia, ... with delusions that he is at times surrounded with guns and fire'. He was returned to the asylum and stayed there till he died in 1906. [11]

A similar unhappy fate awaited Thomas, the fourth son, and Eliza's husband.

moved into his father Matthew's old house in Upper Church. Thomas is described as a cliff farmer in the parish registers, but he had only a small plat, and John Gill implied he did some smuggling.

Thomas and Eliza had three children: Algernon Tom (born 1875), Peter Fred (born 1877) and Lilian Serena (born 1879). But shortly after Lilian's birth, Thomas began to show symptoms of mental illness and was soon committed to Exminster Asylum. His symptoms were quite unlike his brother Matthew's. George Evans notes, dated 11 November 1879, described

> A vacant and despairing appearance. No answer being given to any questions that may be put to him, with entire loss of interest in anything about him, loss of flesh and strength without apparent cause beyond the loss of mind.
>
> About five weeks since he attempted to get out of a window in consequence of being refused to go out and succeeded in doing so, and since the last two or three months a general loss of mind has been observed. Communicated to me by his wife 11.11.1879. [12]

Poor Thomas — he remained in the asylum for sixteen years, and died there in 1895. Poor Eliza! She was thirty-one years old and had three very small children — Algernon aged four, Peter two, and Lilian a few months old. It is not surprising that she was distraught when her husband was certified, sought the aid of a wizard in case he was bewitched, and asked her brother Bill 'to come to her and stop, as she was timid'.

The reality was that she was very vulnerable. She was in an ambiguous situation — still young and good-looking, with no husband, yet neither a widow nor single. Divorce was not yet possible in such cases. When her brother Bill was there he provided company and could chaperone her, but he was mostly away. Her neighbours seem to have been kind. We shall see her discussing her problems with Mrs Northcott and relying on her to look after the children when she was arrested. There was also Mrs Fred Williams, her cousin's wife, 'next door above'. More equivocally, there was David Pile, who lived next door with his family. Eliza said of him: 'I always had regard for him, on account of his being kind to my husband when he was ill'. [13] On the other hand, she had to dismiss him from working her cliff plat. Then, three doors down, there was Amos French with his wife Elizabeth. Amos kept a friendly eye on her but was accused by Pile of making advances to her.

Eliza was not only vulnerable; despite her relatively prosperous in-laws she was also poor. In the census of 1881 she was still described as 'lace-maker', but by then the lace factory at Barnells had closed and sales had declined. She still rented Thomas's cliff plat for 10s a year, and its produce yielded a small income.[14] Bill, while with her, no doubt paid for his keep and probably more. William Williams, her brother-in-law and landlord, may have been understanding about paying the rent. But none of this was enough and she had to apply for 'outdoor relief' under the Poor Law, which involved the humiliation of her name being posted on the Church door. By 1881 the Honiton Poor Law Union was paying her 4s 6d a week because of 'sickness in the family' but by 1884 she was cruelly reclassified as a widow, and the amount was reduced to 4s.[15] Since a Branscombe labourer's wages at the time were 10s a week, and hard enough to live on at that, Eliza must have had great difficulty keeping the household going.

Eliza's lace

Dowell, as we have seen, described Eliza as a 'poor, ignorant country woman', which in educational terms she was. But she comes out of this story as intelligent and feisty, and as a woman who, when angry, could shake her fist in a man's face. She could persuade Bill to come home for tea instead of staying in the pub, and to accompany her to Honiton, for propriety's sake, when he would rather not go. When asked if she wished to testify at the inquest, to clear her name, her reply was careful and clear-headed: 'Of course I wish to, but I don't want to say anything of no consequence. I wish to say what I know, of course. I know nothing of the death of Perryman'.

Amos French

The other accused accomplice was Amos French. He was 52 in 1883, the eldest son of Samuel and Tryphena French, and grew up in a cottage in what is now part of the churchyard. He married Jemima Bucknell when he was 22 and she only 16, but already pregnant with their first child, Mary. Two years later they had another daughter, Margaretta, and then, in 1858, Jemima died, aged only 22. A year later he married Elizabeth Pile, and by 1861, if not before, he was living in the cottage at the east end of Upper Church, where he remained for the rest of his life. Amos and Elizabeth had a further six children, but two of these died within a year of being born, and a third died at the age of seven.

The 1881 census shows them with their three surviving children, Jemima, William and Ellen, and a four-year-old grandson Roland. Roland was the illegitimate son of Mary, Amos's eldest daughter, whom Amos and Elizabeth had simply added to their family — a not infrequent occurrence in the village. Mary had been 'in service' and Roland was baptised Roland John Warren French. The name John Warren, not known in Branscombe, was possibly that of Mary's employer.

At Upper Church Amos and Elizabeth were surrounded by their kith and kin. Next door (west) was Margaretta, the other daughter of Amos's first marriage, with her husband William Wyatt, a sawyer, and their small child. David Pile, who lived beyond the Wyatts, was Elizabeth's younger brother. Amos's sister Harriet, with her husband James Gosling and family, were neighbours to the east, down the road from Upper Church, and his father Samuel French lived with the Goslings until he died in 1882. (see Figure 5.)

Parish registers called Amos 'labourer' until 1870, then he was listed as a cliff farmer. In fact, he rented more land on the cliff than anyone else (he paid £6 annual rent in 1883) and also rented from

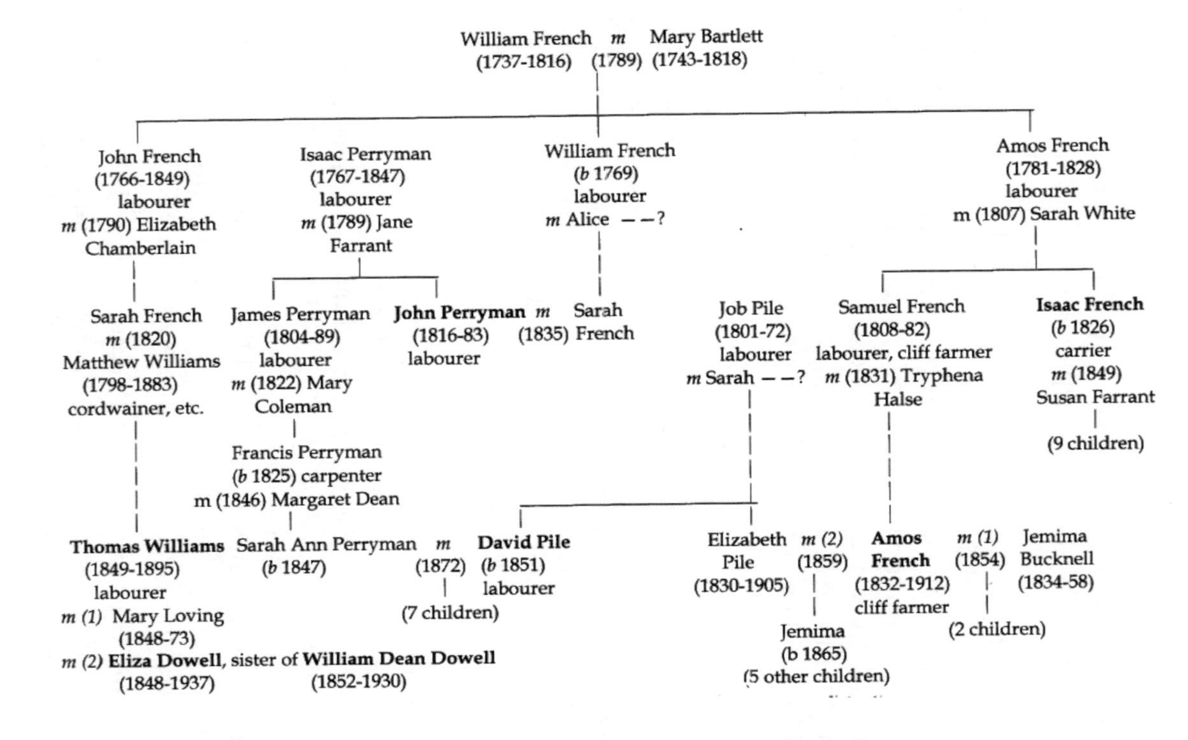

Figure 5: Family connections – Perryman, Dowell, Williams & French

Henry Ford a potato plot in the field behind his house. He kept pigs, so the family was fairly self-sufficient in basic foodstuffs and had an income from market gardening. A newspaper report described him in court as 'comfortably dressed in the style of a small farmer'. [16] Even so, the rest of the family all worked: his wife and daughters were lace-makers and his son, aged 14 in 1881, was a labourer.

On the Saturday of Perryman's death Amos had been to Honiton market, and on his return (in the words of his daughter Jemima) he 'attended to the potatoes in the linhay for the pigs ... he then went to sleep by the fireside'. [17] His piggery was probably on the other side of the road, opposite his front door.

Blocked door of Amos French's piggery

The Perryman case shows Amos French in two contrasted lights. His behaviour throughout fitted the image of a hardworking family man of fairly comfortable means, a teetotaller and a church-goer, content to sleep at his fireside of an evening. He often exhibited an almost phlegmatic calm. When arrested by P. C. Slee he 'replied that he was innocent and ready to go', [18] and when the magistrates discharged him he 'maintained the same calmness which has marked him throughout the proceedings'. [19] On the other hand, the prosecution portrayed him as having had a 'violent quarrel' with his brother-in-law David Pile, of harbouring homicidal intentions and even, perhaps, purloining a gun for such a purpose. What seems clear is that, family man or not, he was attracted to his neighbour Eliza and, though slow to anger, when roused he was willing to fight it out there and then with Pile 'for scandalising his character'. [20]

PART FOUR
THE INQUEST RESUMES

CHAPTER NINE

A Complaint and a Quarrel

In Branscombe school

Mr Cox, the Deputy Coroner, had arranged the second sitting of the inquest for one o'clock on Tuesday, 24 September. In place of the cramped taproom at The Fountain Head, he had obtained the use of the new village schoolroom, to the delight of the children, who were given the afternoon off. Villagers crowded in, mainly women, the men being out in the fields.[1] Once again Henry Ford and the Reverend Swansborough were present, together with John Pyle of Edge Farm.

The Coroner might have assumed that in the two weeks between the first and second sittings the culprit would be apprehended and charged, and a hearing before the magistrates in Honiton would be under way. But the police had not moved that fast. It was twelve days before Bill Dowell and his sister and Amos French were arrested on Thursday 20 September, and when, the next day, they were brought before the chief magistrate, Colonel Graves, Superintendent de Schmid was granted an adjournment to gather more evidence. The following Monday he requested another adjournment, causing Mr Every to protest on behalf of the prisoners:

> The inquest was opened a fortnight ago; and he did expect that that day the Superintendent would have been prepared with some statement that would have assigned reasonable grounds for the detention of the prisoners. At present there was not a fragment of evidence against them. [2]

De Schmid replied that the police had only just discovered a gun and other evidence, so Colonel Graves remanded the prisoners in custody for a further two days until Wednesday 25 September, the day for Petty Sessions.

The Coroner, knowing all this, determined not to delay but to pursue his own inquiry into the cause of Perryman's death. He asked for the three prisoners to be brought under guard from Honiton, and Mr Every came to 'watch the proceedings' on their behalf. De Schmid, already behaving like a prosecutor, was probably glad of the opportunity to rehearse his witnesses and to begin the construction of a case of mistaken identity, in which Dowell's behaviour on the evening of the shooting was to be made to appear suspicious, and a row between Amos French and Pile was to become a motive for killing. Up to now this scenario had featured only in rumours and leaks to the press, but in the course of the afternoon the Coroner elicited its outline, and the three prisoners heard for the first time some of the evidence against them. They were not allowed to speak, though Dowell could not resist interrupting.

From what was said, and from what Dowell wrote in his pamphlet, we can now begin to answer more fully the question of why they were arrested — why, almost from the beginning, they were the prime, and indeed the only, suspects. This chapter explains why the police thought Dowell had a motive for murder, and the next, why they thought he had the means and opportunity.

A journey to Honiton

Having discounted the possibilities that Perryman was the intended victim, or the victim of an accident, the police needed to find someone with a motive to kill a person for whom Perryman might have been mistaken.

It so happened that news of a Branscombe quarrel had been brought to the Honiton police station on the very day of the shooting, for on the afternoon of September 8th Eliza Williams went there to lodge a complaint against her neighbour David Pile for using threatening language towards her. So once it was known that Pile was working at Edge Farm with Perryman, the police might have wondered if an ambush had been laid for him on the homeward path, which went wrong when Perryman was mistaken for Pile. Eliza, to be sure, was an unlikely gunman, but her brother William Dowell had accompanied her to Honiton, and police records probably showed that he had held a license to shoot the previous year.

According to Dowell, he had in fact only heard about Pile's threats to Eliza two days before, when she asked him to accompany her to Honiton to have Pile bound over to keep the peace. Dowell agreed to go, 'I being her brother and her husband being in the asylum', but reluctantly, since Pile was a friend with whom he had 'never had an angry word'. [3] Eliza confirmed that

> he was on good terms with David Pile when he went to Honiton for a summons, but he said he would go with me for my protection. He said I should have to pay for it and that he wouldn't give me a penny towards it. [4]

Once in Honiton, however, Eliza and her brother were inevitably seen as acting together, so the police could easily have perceived them as partners in crime.

In search of a lawyer, they went first to Mr Every's office to see if a warrant could be obtained against Pile, binding him over to keep the peace. Every's clerk took them to the office of the Magistrate's Clerk, Mr E. Stamp, who said a warrant would be inappropriate because ten days had passed since the alleged threats were made, but he told them they could have a summons if they wished. When they decided against that, Stamp advised them to ask Honiton police to communicate with P. C. Martin at Branscombe, with a view to warning Pile of serious consequences if there were threats in future. Eliza thanked him for this suggestion and spoke accordingly to Sergeant Jeffery at the police station, who agreed to her request. Dowell says they 'left Honiton highly pleased with our mission, as [Eliza] considered it the best and cheapest way' [5] and they returned to Branscombe in the horse-drawn van of Isaac French the carrier (Plate 10).

When Martin told the inquest about his nocturnal walk with Dowell after the shooting, he tried to give the impression that he had already become suspicious of his companion. He said he had asked Dowell where he had been all evening and whether he could account for himself. The reporter noted that 'Dowell here laughed' — presumably at Martin's attempt to present himself as a sleuth on the scent, rather than a bewildered village bobby clutching at straws. But Dowell was not amused when Martin used this to introduce a slanted reference to the altercation between Eliza and Pile, stating that Dowell had replied

> "I never left home all the evening after I come home from Honiton, where I'd been with my sister to get a summons for Pile". He added, "You know what it is for; it's about the row we had the other night; and I expect you will have a letter about it on Monday morning". [6]

In his pamphlet, Dowell scoffed:

> the *row* we had ... How was it possible for me to say such a thing when I had never heard an angry word between my sister and Pyle in my whole life, nor had one myself. [7]

Sergeant Jeffery's letter duly arrived on Monday, and Every extracted its contents from Martin despite the Superintendent's objections:

Martin: The nature of the communication was that David Pyle, of Branscombe, had threatened Eliza Williams with a hook.
Every: Was there any instruction given by P. S. Jeffery as to Pile?

Here de Schmid intervened:

de Schmid: I object to that question.
Every: Upon what ground?
de Schmid: Because it does not bear on the matter.
Every (to the Coroner): Will you take note of that?
Coroner: I take no notes of objections.

Why did de Schmid object? Because Every, who was no fool, was touching on a weak point in the police case, one which he was bound to press harder when acting for the defence in court. If the prosecution argument was that the quarrel led to the shooting,

Every needed to establish exactly what had happened in Honiton. He said he intended to subpoena a witness who would tell the inquest that Mrs Williams had been perfectly satisfied with the outcome of her visit to the police. The Coroner then allowed him to continue, and de Schmid reluctantly withdrew his objection.

Martin explained that the letter instructed him to warn Pile that if he continued to threaten Mrs Williams he would render himself liable to arrest, and that he was to give Mrs Williams police protection. One can understand de Schmid's defensiveness. If the police had dealt with Eliza's complaints to her entire satisfaction, what possible reason could there be for Dowell to shoot Pile the same evening? At the next session of the inquest de Schmid was to make a crude attempt to plug this gap in his case.

The quarrel

When he received the letter from Honiton, Martin would have pieced together Eliza's claim that David Pile had threatened her, with the recent quarrel he already knew about, between Pile and Amos French, which also concerned Eliza. A vivid picture of this quarrel can be obtained from evidence given to this session of the inquest and the next, when Eliza was allowed to give evidence herself.

Eliza's difficulties with Pile went back more than a year. When her husband Thomas was committed to the asylum in 1879 she retained the cliff plat which he rented and employed her neighbour David Pile, who also had a cliff plat, to work it for her. But in the spring of 1882 she cancelled this arrangement and asked Samuel Coombes, a sixty-three-year-old labourer from Street and a devout Methodist, to tend it instead. David Pile was upset, and, according to Eliza, for the next eighteen months he showed 'ill-feeling towards her'.

This brings us to July 1883, and the night of Honiton fair. As Eliza tells it:

> I was in my garden, which was next to Pile's. Pile was in his garden, and he commenced to use bad language towards me.

He had a hook in his hand, with which he was beating down a bed of onions. He said 'I should like to "do" for you with this'.[8]

Later, Pile swore on oath that he had never threatened her life, or threatened her with a hook. Whether he did or did not, the abuse continued, and at the beginning of September it took a new turn. He started to insinuate that she and her neighbour Amos French were getting 'friendly'. He said

I saw Amos French place some groceries in a secret place at the back of the cottages, and soon afterwards she walked straight there and took possession of them. [9]

This hint of a secret intrigue meant that Amos was bound to get involved, and matters finally came to a head on the Thursday evening before the death of Perryman, i.e. on September 6th.

Pile had been working at Edge Farm since the middle of July, and on that day he apparently came home from harvesting by the main village road from Street. Harvesting went on until eight o'clock, so by the time he reached home it was about a quarter to nine. The scene which followed must be imagined taking place in darkness, with the road outside the houses partially lit by the moon and by lamplight from cottage doors and windows.

Eliza was outside her house washing out a milk-can, and as David Pile came up he said, 'You ought to be in an asylum, like your husband; how about Amos French?' According to Eliza, she went back into her house without replying. Questioned further by the Coroner, she explained that:

Eliza: About half an hour afterwards French passed my door, and went into his own house close by, and said to his wife 'What has Eliza been crying about?' A few minutes afterwards he came into my house, and said 'What has David been saying about me?' I told him.

Coroner: Did French, in your presence, use any threats towards Pile?

Eliza: No; he did not answer. [10]

David Pile took up the story:

> *Pile:* I saw Amos French coming out of Mrs Williams' house, and French said 'What have you to say about me?' I replied 'Nothing in particular'. French offered me 2s. if I would knock him, but I refused to do so. French then said 'I would as soon die as live for 'ee'.

Further questioning elicited more detail — Amos took off his coat when he offered to fight, and Eliza came out and accused Pile of saying that she and Amos were always talking together. She even 'shook her fist in my face' said Pile, 'and accused me of having called her an improper name'.

By now neighbours and relations had gathered round. When the dispute was going on, William Wyatt, son-in-law to Amos French, was present, and he said 'he should like to give Pile something' — meaning, presumably, a punch. David Pile's wife Sarah Ann testified that besides Eliza, French's wife Elizabeth and both Wyatts were present. She said the row was opposite her house, implying that she could hear and see what was going on without stepping outside. But if Sarah Ann had gone out to support her husband, she would have been insulted to her face by Amos, who, according to Pile, said she was seen to 'come out of a drangway on the Monday previous with another man'. [11]

The confrontation probably did not last very long, and the participants traded nothing worse than insults. Everyone agrees that Bill Dowell was not there, and it seems that by the time he arrived home the protagonists were all indoors. He was greeted by an enraged Eliza: 'David Pile has been calling me dreadful names; I will go to Honiton on Saturday to see whether I cannot make him prove his words or withdraw them'. [12] David Pile had much the same idea: he went off to find P. C. Martin and asked him whether French could not be made to 'prove his allegation about Mrs Pile'. Martin said he would 'speak to French about it'. The next morning Pile was back again complaining to Martin that 'Wyatt ... called his little girl [only nine years of age] an offensive name'.

It is striking that although French lost his temper he still offered to pay Pile to hit him first, to provide the pretext for a fight. This gives their confrontation a touch of formality, like a duel in which honour required him to defend an injured reputation. Pile refused the challenge; he had no stomach for a fight with his brother-in-law or for the family feud that would ensue. In court, the police tried to make mileage out of French's obscure remark — 'I would as soon die as live for 'ee' — as if by 'die' he meant 'hang' and was therefore threatening Pile's life, but it was made clear that he only said it in the heat of the moment. French rather sheepishly admitted that he did threaten Pile, but claimed that:

> I had never threatened him in that way before. I should not have done so then, but I was angry with him for scandalising my character in saying that he had seen me and Mrs Williams close together, which was wrong. [13]

And Pile agreed that French would not 'have said what he did unless he was in a passion, and he wanted to fight out the quarrel there and then'.

It appears from Dowell's account that Eliza and Pile had kept their animosity to themselves until it became public that Thursday evening, and he was reluctant to side with his sister against his friend. Even Eliza denied that she bore Pile any ill-will for what he had been saying about her, claiming that 'I only wished him to stop it'. [14] The fact that both Eliza and Pile went to someone in authority suggests they wanted to cool things. If, as intended, both Pile and French had been admonished, peace might have been restored. Instead of which, Perryman was shot two days later, and the police turned the 'row' into the cornerstone of their murder theory. But it was a shaky foundation, for Dowell claimed that

> On the Sunday I was in the cells, I was told there was a detective in [Pile's] house, almost trying to make him swear that there had been a quarrel between him and me, but he told them he was sure that there never had. [15]

And indeed no evidence was produced that there had been.

We have gone along with what was said about the quarrel at the inquest, but we have to recognise that the three defendants would have wanted to minimize its significance. Yet David Pile, their supposed victim, had no such interest, so why was he also unwilling to make much of it? He may have had his own reasons, for there is a strong whiff of sexual rivalry that he may not have wanted made public.

Reading between the lines, it is easy to imagine that Pile was infatuated with his next-door neighbour. Eliza was 35 and on her own; he was 32, his wife was seven years older, and, if there was any truth in the aspersion cast on Sarah Ann Pile's fidelity, there may have been strains in his marriage. When, during the inquest, Eliza mentioned dismissing David Pile from her cliff plat, she also denied — in answer to an unreported question that the Coroner put to her — that there had been any improper intimacy between them. But Pile may well have made unwelcome advances which she did not want repeated, and this could be why she replaced him with the innocuous Coombes. Pile's continuing bitterness against her may reflect the frustration and humiliation of a rejected lover; certainly his insinuations against French suggest jealousy.

Eliza was also asked about her relationship with Amos French, and again insisted there had been no improper intimacy between them. French clearly felt protective towards Eliza, but at 52 he might have had a soft spot for a younger woman and his protectiveness may have been less than innocent. If there was a hidden drama of sexual competition between Eliza's two neighbours, it might even have sparked off murderous thoughts. It looks as if the Coroner was pursuing such a theory of *crime passionnel* when he questioned Eliza about her sexual conduct towards Pile and French, which would have pointed towards Amos as the more likely murderer.

But the police, having fixed on Dowell as the murderer, could not then accuse French of lying in ambush for Pile. A theory of sexual rivalry could add little to their case, for no jury would believe that French had persuaded Dowell to shoot Pile *for* him. The police must have considered that Dowell's own protectiveness towards his sister was, however improbably, a sufficient motive for murdering Pile.

But if French had a sexual motive for wanting Pile out of the way, he could have been an accessory to a murder planned by Dowell, and this was probably why he was arrested.

The Coroner was to conclude, after hearing all the evidence, that 'he was unable to see any sufficient motive on [Dowell's] part to induce him to murder Pile'. So once again we are left wondering whether Martin was swept along by the wave of village speculation; or whether Dowell's guilt was partly the brainchild of Superintendent de Schmid and Martin simply went along with his superior; or again, as hinted at darkly by Dowell, whether he was bribed to perjure himself.

CHAPTER TEN

Means and Opportunity

This chapter continues with the second sitting of the inquest, on September 25, and deals with two questions which it tried to answer: did Dowell have access to a gun? And would David Pile's homeward path from Edge Farm have offered an opportunity to waylay and shoot him? There was to be more evidence and argument on both these questions at later sittings of the inquest, and for completeness' sake we shall bring some of it forward into this discussion.

Post mortem report

George Evans, the surgeon, was the first witness called when the inquest resumed, and he presented, a little pompously, his findings from the *post mortem*:

> He found on opening the chest, where the greater part of the charge had been received, a considerable effusion under the skin. There were also indications of a lung having been wounded. The pericardium was half full of blood. The two shots had gone through the right ventricle and the pulmonary artery. That, together with the wound in the upper part of the lung, accounts for the blood flowing from the mouth and was the immediate cause of death. The shot which was the cause of death he found in the pericardium. He found other shots in the chest. [1]

He then produced several shots from the body, and was questioned in an attempt to fix the distance and position from which the gun was fired:

> *De Schmid:* Do you think that the shot entered the body at any great distance from a firearm?

Evans: I should judge that the shot must have been fired at a distance from 25 to 30 yards.

Every: Do I understand you to say that the shots were fired immediately in front of the deceased?

Evans: I have not the least doubt of it.

Every: Then, may we assume that the person who fired the shot was in front?

Evans: Yes, or somewhat to the left.

Every: Then you say that the shots took an upward direction from left to right?

Evans: Yes. There were no shots on the legs.

Other evidence shows that Evans meant 'left' to be understood from the point of view of the person firing the gun. The absence of shot in the legs is consistent with a newspaper report that Perryman was shot as he came up out of a hollow, which could be significant in considering whether he was shot by accident.

The *Exeter Flying Post* report added another detail — Evans thought the weapon was probably an ordinary shot gun. [2] By this time double-barrels had become the sporting guns of gentry and farmers, but an ordinary shot gun used by villagers would still be a single-barrelled muzzle-loader. Evans's findings indicate that Perryman received the charge from one barrel, in all likelihood from a single-barrelled gun.

In search of a murder weapon

It was on Monday, the day before this second sitting of the inquest, that de Schmid told Colonel Graves that the police had found a gun — of which more in Chapter 12. Up to that point they had failed to find a possible murder weapon. At the scene of the shooting Martin had found only a small piece of brown paper, which was never mentioned again or explained. Wider searches of Culverwell Hill found no discarded gun, hardly surprising given the limited manpower available to search a wilderness of pits, some dating back more than a century and thickly overgrown.

Martin versus Dowell: the question of the gun

The police's suspicions of Dowell were partly suggested, or confirmed, by finding that he had taken out a gun license in 1882, and they assumed this meant he owned a gun. As with the quarrel, P. C. Martin used the chance offered by his unwitnessed night-walk with Dowell over Culverwell Hill to give a tendentious and damaging account of their conversation about guns. Not surprisingly, hearing this version of events, Dowell became 'very excited, and frequently interrupted the proceedings'. As he said later: 'Reader, put it to yourself how you would have felt when your friend, as you thought, was trying to swear your life away falsely'. [3] In presenting Martin's evidence we not only reproduce Dowell's interruptions, but interpolate italicised quotations from his pamphlet, refuting Martin's allegations.

Martin began:

> Dowell went with me some of the way, and on the road he remarked, 'It must be someone who did it that keeps guns. I don't know very many who keep guns barring myself, young Power and Mr Gill.' Continuing, he said 'It could not be me, because I have not my gun at home. My gun is up to Dunscombe, at my brother-in-law's. He took it with him when he changed houses.'

Referring to this conversation, Dowell wrote in his pamphlet 'And here I charge Martin with several deliberate lies' — first, that he had ever said there were only three guns in the village; and secondly, that he had said that one of them was his:

> *A cursed liar! When my name was on the church door at the same time as the holder of a gun license for 1882 in the midst of 20 or 30 more ... As regards myself, I never had a gun in my life of my own. The old one I used to fire with sometimes belonged to my brother-in-law. ... The last time I fired a gun was in May 1883.* [4]

John Collier, the brother-in-law whose gun Dowell admits having used, had indeed gone to live at Dunscombe, in the neighbouring parish of Salcombe Regis, earlier in 1883. Though Dowell insisted that the gun Collier took there was Collier's, not his, he did not deny that he told Martin about it on their walk. And two days later Martin paid a visit to Dunscombe:

> On Monday night, the 10th inst., about ten o'clock, I again saw Dowell. He was coming out of the Fountain Head inn with several others. About twenty minutes afterwards, Dowell, addressing me, said 'I don't much like it, Martin, as I've been told that you've been out to my sister's to inquire about my gun, and you've much frightened her.'

We can hear, through Martin's words, Dowell's indignation that Martin had thought it necessary to check up on his story. Since nothing more was ever said about this visit, we can assume that Martin found that Dowell had been telling the truth. Nevertheless, whether in good faith or bad, Martin still wanted the inquest to hear how he pursued the question of whether Dowell had a gun, so he continued:

> I asked Dowell whether he had a gun in his house then, or any powder and shot. He replied 'I have no gun; I told you where my gun was.'

In his pamphlet Dowell pointed out that at the time Martin was misrepresenting him at the inquest his statements had already been corroborated elsewhere:

> *The prosecution knew I had no gun, because a man in the village whom I told them of, had asked me twice for the loan of the old gun that I used to carry, when I told him my brother-in-law had left the parish and taken the old gun with him in June before the old man was shot in September, and they went to this man and found that what I said was quite right; and if I had been carrying a gun, I should have had a license the same as the year before.*[5]

Up to this point, therefore, the police's suspicion that Dowell had access to a gun remained just that, suspicion, and they had to make what they could of the fact that he had used a gun in the past. If Dowell is to be believed — and he is perfectly consistent — Martin deliberately slanted his evidence to imply that Dowell must have a gun hidden somewhere. And very belatedly, after Dowell had been arrested, they searched Eliza's house:

> *There came two or three fellows, who turned our house upside down. They turned my best clothes out on the floor, and served our beds the same, and there they left them. It was shameful how they served the property. They had it all to themselves, and what they were looking for, I cannot tell.* [6]

Presumably they still hoped to find a gun.

Martin versus Dowell: powder and shot

On the Monday evening after the shooting, according to Martin, he and Dowell walked down the road from the Fountain Head to Eliza's house. Dowell told his sister to show Martin a powder flask and shot belt which, Martin said, 'belonged to Dowell' — but which Dowell said in his pamphlet 'belonged to my brother-in-law'. At this point in his evidence Martin began to hesitate. He said that he had given some of the shot and powder to de Schmid. He then produced 'two ordinary flasks' for the Coroner and jury to look at, but on being questioned further, admitted he

> could not tell whether it was the same from which I took a portion when at Dowell's house, and which I had handed to the Superintendent ...

Dowell interrupted to confirm that 'It is the same'. The Coroner then turned to de Schmid:

> *Coroner:* Can you produce the shot which you took away from Dowell's house?
>
> *De Schmid*: I have the shot, but unfortunately I left it behind at Honiton.
>
> *Coroner [clearly exasperated]:* Well, there is no doubt that this inquiry will not be concluded this day, so that the

> jury will have an opportunity of seeing the shot in question another time.

Martin and de Schmid may have been prevaricating, hoping the jury would not compare the shot from Eliza's house with the shot removed from Perryman's body by Evans until they were sure the comparison would stand up in the magistrates' court next day. If so, they were probably relieved when the Coroner did not persist.

Under further questioning, Martin agreed that the shot flask was the same as the one that Eliza took down from her dresser and gave him. He recalled that while he was examining the shot, Dowell had pointed out that there were two different sizes, which he found to be correct. He went on:

> Dowell then said, 'Poor George Williams, I lent it to him, and he must have mixed it.' [7] Before I left Dowell's house he said, 'I am innocent. You may depend you are on the wrong scent.' I said, 'I hope I am'.

At this Dowell interrupted again:

> *Dowell*: Are those the same words?
> *Coroner (to Dowell):* I cannot allow you to interrupt.
> *P. S. Jeffery (to Dowell):* You have your legal adviser if you want to ask any questions.
> *Dowell here made some remark as to the powder and shot.*
> *Every (to Dowell):* You must keep order, or take the case yourself.
> *Dowell*: Well, I like to hear the truth.

Why was Dowell so upset? Was it just because Martin had said 'George' instead of 'Thomas'? Or, more to the point, because he had omitted one vital fact:

> *When my sister gave the shot belt and powder flask to Martin without being asked for them they were an eighth of an inch thick in dust, as they had been on the top of the shelves several months without having been touched.*

A Pile of confusions

Knowing about the quarrel with David Pile and suspecting that Dowell had access to a gun, Martin must have been impressed by the ease and speed with which someone living at Upper Church could reach the site of the ambush, and then escape. This scenario depended, of course, on the murderer believing that Pile, the intended victim, would use the path through Old Pits — but who better placed than Dowell, Eliza and French, his close neighbours, to know his movements? However David Pile proved to be a nightmare of a witness from the police's point of view.

De Schmid tried hard to make Pile admit that he often came home by the same path that Perryman took on the fatal night. Pile first said that he had not been that way three times in the last year, then in the last six months, then 'I do not think I have come that way this harvest'. In answer to Every, he agreed that whichever way he came he 'almost always had company'. But then he admitted that he might have come back via the Pits on his own during the past six months!

Every returned to the quarrel, this time to establish that Amos French's threats were made in the heat of the moment. Pile got his drift and said, yes, Amos wanted 'to fight out the quarrel there and then'; and no, Bill Dowell was not there during the quarrel, and no, Dowell would have no reason to believe he was coming home by way of the Pits on the night of the 8th. Unfortunately at least one of the jury did not believe him:

Mr John Ellis (a juryman): Did you pass over Culverwell Hill any night during the week that Perriman was shot?
Pile: I can't remember; I don't think I did.

On being further questioned, Pile said he knew that he did not walk over the Pits during the week alluded to. The questioning was becoming a free-for-all, so P. C. Martin had a go, suggesting he had come over Culverwell Hill twice during the week previous to Perryman's death. But Pile still denied it.

On this unsatisfactory note the Coroner decided to adjourn the inquest, since it was now seven o'clock, but to recall Pile at the next sitting, which he appointed for the following Monday, October 1st. What passed on that occasion will be discussed in Chapter 12, but this is a convenient place to round off the Coroner's further attempts to get a clear and consistent answer from Pile as to whether he had recently come home over Culverwell Hill:

Coroner: You stated at the former inquest that you knew positively that you did not come by night over Culverwell Hill during the five days previously to the day Perryman was shot. You also stated that ... you did not come that way at any time during this harvest before the death of Perryman. Are those statements correct? Did you come over Culverwell Hill by night during the five days before Perryman was shot?

Pile: No, sir, not that week; but I did the week before ... I don't believe I have twice. [8]

One of the jury still thought he knew better:

William Pike (a juryman): Did you not tell me that you went over the Pits path on Culverwell Hill on the night of the murder, and afterwards deny it?

Pile: That was the Thursday before.

William Pike: I know what you told me; I am not a child.

Finally, in answer to the Coroner, Pile said that he did come home with Perryman on Thursday September 6 (two days before the shooting, and the night of the quarrel) but that they came down the main road. He seems to have meant that on that Thursday Perryman did not take his usual short cut through Old Pits but that the two of them continued over Culverwell Hill by Pit lane to Street and then came down the main village road. If so, Pile would have had to pass Eliza's house before reaching his own, and would have seen her washing out a milk-can at her door, as she testified.

There the matter rested. It is far from clear whether Pile admitted *ever* coming home by the path through Old Pits. But if nothing else, his evidence suggested that his habits were too inconstant for a would-be murderer to be able to count on his taking a particular track as a settled routine. Nor did the Coroner ask any of the three accused if *they* thought he would come through Old Pits on the night of September 8th. Pile also said that 'The reason he had for using the paths which he generally walked over was because he usually had company that way'. If he disliked walking home alone at night he would hardly be a suitable target for an ambush.

PART FIVE
CASE DISMISSED BUT UNRESOLVED

CHAPTER ELEVEN

Before the Bench

At eleven o'clock on Wednesday 26 September, many of those who had attended the second sitting of the inquest in Branscombe the night before made their way to Honiton police court, ten miles by cart or on foot. This was to be the moment of reckoning. At last the magistrates were to hear the case against William Dowell, Eliza Williams and Amos French, and might send one or more of them for trial at the next Assizes, where, if convicted, the murderer would be condemned to death. The Petty Sessions Room (which no longer exists) was crowded with people from Honiton as well as Branscombe and many who could not gain admittance remained outside the front entrance. [1]

The prisoners were accommodated with chairs and, somewhat surprisingly, appeared cheerful. No doubt they were buoyed up by the presence of many well-wishers, by the prospect of finally having a say, by faith in their own innocence, and by the words of Psalm 35.

The magistrates, having retired after discharging the routine business of Petty Sessions — licenses, jury lists, etc. — returned to the bench. Colonel Graves, the chairman, was flanked by Major Speid and Lord Sidmouth, who was apt to pull rank and assume the role of spokesman. The police had entrusted the prosecution to an Exeter solicitor, Mr Toby. The accused were again defended by Mr Every. Dowell, who had probably been strictly instructed not to interrupt, 'took great interest in the proceedings' and 'frequently supplied notes, as the evidence was being taken'.

Toby opened by outlining the theory of the prosecution, namely:

> that it was the intention of someone to shoot a labourer named Pile, and not the deceased. A gun had been found in

a linhay, and from indications it appeared that the gun had been recently fired.

He said he felt sure that, although the case 'was shrouded in mystery', the magistrates would 'if they considered that a *prima facie* [i.e. reasonable] case was established, send one or more of the prisoners for trial'. His slightly half-hearted words showed awareness that the case he was about to present was less than compelling, and no doubt he was hoping to persuade the bench to set a low threshold for its acceptance as evidence of guilt.

The principal witnesses at the inquest testified once again, in very similar terms. Loveridge covered Perryman's last walk home from Edge Farm and his departure in the direction of Old Pits; Tidwell described finding Perryman, and his last moments; David Pile yet again tried to explain his ways home from work and described the quarrel with French, to which Mrs Pile added detail. Then came the official witnesses, on whom the burden of the case rested: Evans, repeating his *post-mortem* findings, then Martin and de Schmid, who tried to present a detailed circumstantial case regarding means and opportunity. In this chapter we will pick out those issues that have not been discussed before.

Waistcoats on and off

A new focus of interest was on whether the working clothes worn by Perryman and Pile would have made them easy to mistake by moonlight. Loveridge said that on the night in question Perryman wore 'a light jacket, a darkish waistcoat, and a dark pair of trousers', and Pile confirmed that he also had worn a light coloured coat and dark trousers, but with a light waistcoat. [2] Loveridge added that Perryman did not always wear dark trousers, and Sarah Anne Pile pointed out that her husband's trousers were much darker than Perryman's usual light-coloured corduroys. The pale coat was the main point in the prosecution's favour, and Toby could have (but did not) point out that Perryman's trousers were probably hidden from the gunman as he came up out of a hollow towards him, since no shot was found in his legs.

Every tried again for a less confused account of Pile's homeward route than had emerged at the inquest, but met with little success. Pile's offering this time was as follows:

> It depended on the part of the farm at which I was at work which way I came home ... I have been over Culverwell Hill lately, but not within a week of Perryman's death. The week before Perryman's death I walked over Culverwell Hill, although I stated at the inquest that I had not. I have slept since and remembered more. I know that I had not been over Culverwell Hill during the third week previous to Perryman's death ... I cannot recollect that I had been over Culverwell Hill more than once for three weeks before Perryman's death.

Toby voiced his suspicion that Pile had been coached and, being an interloper from Exeter, promptly got a rap on the knuckles from Lord Sidmouth:

> *Toby:* Were you examined by Mr Every after you were summoned?
>
> *Pile:* No, Sir.
>
> *Every:* I state distinctly that I have not seen this witness, only at the Coroner's inquest.
>
> *Sidmouth:* This never ought to have come before us; we know Mr Every.

When Pile seemed to admit that he came home over Culverwell Hill on the night of the quarrel, Toby, ignorant of the lie of the land, asked whether French might have seen him coming that way, but Pile only replied, reasonably enough, 'I do not know'.

Every drew from Sarah Ann Pile a further detail as to waistcoats — in this case, that Amos French's mysterious threat — 'I would as soon die as live for you' — had been uttered when not only his coat had been thrown off, but his waistcoat too, and therefore 'when he was in a high passion'. He was not, in other words, expressing a settled intention to kill. This left open, of course, the possibility that he might have developed such an intention while brooding on the matter afterwards.

The trespassers' path

So far then, the answers as to who was wearing what, and whether the assailant would really have expected Pile to come home via the Old Pits, had proved inconclusive. The prosecution now focussed on how someone living at Upper Church could have quickly reached, and left, the scene of the crime without being visible from the road.

We think we know where Perryman was shot, and our reasoning is in Appendix B. If we are right, the gun was fired from a position on what was then a scrubby grass hillside above the upper, north-western boundary of Culverwell Hill Coppice (see map, Figure 3, p.28). The person who fired would have been looking uphill towards a low bank over which Perryman's path brought him out of the Old Pits. P. C. Martin, who now took the stand, told the magistrates

> I went to the spot where Perryman was killed, and saw some powder there. I saw a place where apparently someone had been lying down. The furze and brambles were bent down ... A man lying at the spot where the brambles were crushed five minutes would cause such an impression as he saw the following morning after Perrryman was killed.

He then described a track going away from this spot in the direction of Upper Church, which he called 'the six cottages':

> I traced a track from the spot where the impression was on the ground through the furze to the Collick, which is the name for several potato plots belonging to many persons, among whom is French, but I couldn't distinguish the marks. The track was in the direction of the six cottages ... The path throughout the undergrowth from where the impression on the ground was he should call a trespassers' path. I traced the tracks as far as behind Perryman's house.

We believe this track to be a disused footpath that runs downhill from Old Pits through Culverwell Hill Coppice. Martin presumably called it a 'trespassers' path' because the coppice and the field beyond were private property. At the south-eastern, bottom end of the Coppice the path comes to a large sloping field which contained allotments, and had once been part of a small farm called Collick's. A person leaving the crime scene this way would have skirted round the lower edge of the allotments to the road entrance — a drangway between Collick's Cottage and the uppermost cottage in Upper Church (Northcott's cottage).[3]

Clearly it would have taken someone living in Upper Church only a few minutes to walk fast up round the field and through the Coppice to the 'impression', and fewer minutes still to run back down. In doing so they would have passed behind Grapevine, at the corner of the field, as mentioned by Martin. He and de Schmid gave various estimates amounting to about four minutes for the time it took them to walk from the impression to Grapevine, and from Grapevine to Northcott's cottage. The estimates seem a bit low to us, but these were very active men, and they are consistent with our notion of where Perryman was shot.

As evidence linking Dowell — or for that matter, any of the residents of Upper Church or Collick's Cottage — to the killing of Perryman, the signs of someone having used the trespassers' path were merely circumstantial, and their force was weakened by the failure to prove that Pile was either likely, or thought likely, to be coming home that way.

The gun from a linhay

P. C. Martin continued with his evidence and was asked about the shot found at Eliza's house. Then his great moment arrived:

Martin: I produce a gun. *(Sensation)*

Or, as another report put it, 'a great commotion was created in court'.[4] Then:

P. S. Jeffrey: Silence!
Martin: I found it in a linhay in Abbot's Hole, on the top of the cliff, about a mile from where Perryman was shot. The linhay belongs to Henry Parrett. Amos French has a linhay near, about two or three paces off.

One can imagine, at this point, how villagers and magistrates alike must have immediately made a connection between Amos French, the gun and the murder. However, Martin somewhat muffed it by continuing:

> *Martin*: Anyone could get at either of the linhays, as there is communication from one to the other ... Anyone could see [the gun] from the outside, as there was a gate to the linhay and not a door.

So not necessarily Amos, after all — anyone could have seen the gun and taken it. Martin confused the issue further by admitting that he himself had *not* actually seen the gun from the outside. (So had he been tipped-off?) He went on:

> There was some powder in a bottle under the linhay, some caps, and a few shot. I took some of the shot away, and part of the powder, which I have left at home. The linhay was used for potatoes, and the gun was on the potatoes on the top shelf. I found the gun last Saturday. It was unloaded. I should say that the gun had been discharged lately, during the past month. There was a percussion cap on the gun. The cap had been exploded, I took away the cap, but it is at home. [5]

At this point the revelation of the gun, which should have been a moment of triumph for the prosecution, turned to anticlimax since Martin had left all the relevant evidence — shot, powder and cap — at home.

Perhaps with good reason, Toby refrained from pressing him for details, and Every, immediately scenting — or probably already knowing — that this reluctance concealed a major weakness in the prosecution case, began his cross-examination. Martin revealed that 'I have had a conversation with [Mr Parrett] about the gun' but then had to admit that 'Mr Parrett is not here' — a strong indication that the conversation had not gone the way he or the prosecution would have liked. Under further questioning he also admitted that Parrett, 'a shoemaker and a highly respectable man', had told him that he had put the gun in the linhay about two years ago. Every then asked twice if Parrett had said (as Every must have known he had) that he had fired the gun off six weeks ago, but Martin twice denied it.

Realising that the prosecution had decided not to expose Parrett to cross-examination, Every then turned innocently on Mr Toby: 'I suppose, Mr Toby, you will call Mr Parrett?' to which Toby coolly replied 'No; I shall not do that'. Lord Sidmouth then gave his opinion that Martin's conversation with Parrett could not be treated as evidence in Parrett's absence, so the significance of the gun from the linhay was left untested and uncertain.

Two sizes of shot

Toby, perhaps beginning to lose heart, returned to the question of the shot found in Perryman's body and bag, and at Dowell's house. George Evans the surgeon, repeating the findings of the *post mortem,* produced six small shots, two of which had passed through Perryman's heart. Every, keeping alive the possibility of a poaching accident, asked if the wounds could have been caused by the accidental discharge of a gun by someone else, and Evans affirmed that they could.

P. C. Martin said that he had compared the shots taken from Dowell's flask with shot lodged in the bag that Perryman was carrying when killed. He repeated that there were two sizes of shot in the flask, but Toby did not ask him how they compared with those from the bag. Superintendent de Schmid, following Martin into the witness box, sounded more definite:

> I searched Eliza Williams' cottage on Thursday — the day on which the prisoners were taken into custody. Mrs Northcott, a neighbour, was in the house in charge for Williams. I found the powder flask and shot flask produced on a dresser in Williams' house. I have compared the shot handed me by the Coroner with shot in the flask. Some correspond. There are two sizes in the shot pouch, and different sizes of shot were found in the body by the doctor, and also in the bag alluded to by P. C. Martin. *(Here the bag alluded to was produced; on a portion of it there was a large spot of blood.)*

But instead of establishing a match between Dowell's shot and that found in the bag or in the body, de Schmid concluded only with the unsurprising finding that 'The shot produced by Martin, taken from the bag, corresponded with some of the shot in the body'.

Every, who at the inquest could only cross-examine de Schmid's witnesses, now had the chance to cross-examine *him*. First, he asked about the shot from the body. The Superintendent said he believed it was of two sizes, but would not swear to it. Colonel Graves interposed that 'it was quite a matter of opinion as to the size of the shot. Unless weighed, he didn't consider that the difference in size could be ascertained'. De Schmid replied that the shot in the flask were fives and sixes. Every then asked him to show the court the difference, and de Schmid handed over shots which he said were 'of two different sizes', although when asked if he would swear to it, he declined. The following smouldering exchanges followed:

Every: Can these shots be distinguished with certainty? You are a military man and an expert, you know.
De Schmid: That has nothing to do with the case.
Every: Can they be distinguished with certainty?
De Schmid: I would not swear, but I can see a difference ...

Every hinted at the possibility of malpractice by de Schmid by requesting that the shot might be sealed up and labelled. Mr Toby 'thought this most unnecessary'.

Chairman: The shot have already been in several hands and they cannot hurt by going into others.
Every: They have been traced regularly from the Coroner to this Court, and I simply ask that as they are extremely delicate to manipulate to have them sealed.
De Schmid: I have to produce the shot at the Coroner's Inquest next Monday.
Chairman: Then we cannot order that it shall be sealed.

Charged and discharged

With the shot, as with the gun, and with the trespassers' path, much less than a *prima facie* case had so far been established. But that was all there was. Mr Toby announced that the case for the prosecution was complete, and the evidence was then read over. The prisoners were charged, and all firmly declared their innocence.

It was now nearly six-thirty. It had been a long day, and after the suspense of listening to questions and answers whose significance was hard to follow yet charged with fateful consequences, 'there was great excitement in Court. One young man was carried out in a fainting condition'.

Every, no doubt expecting that the court would be adjourned and that he would then present the case for the defence, stood up and addressed the bench.

'There are a number of witnesses — '

'One moment, please', interrupted Lord Sidmouth, and the magistrates retired to consult. When they returned the Chairman announced

'The Bench are of opinion that the evidence does not connect the prisoners, and decline to commit them. Therefore they are discharged.'

Suddenly it was all over. None of the three would hang after all!

> There was loud applause in Court on the bench giving their decision. Dowell and Williams seemed to be overjoyed, but Amos French maintained the same calmness which has marked him throughout the proceedings. Dowell cried, and said he was never so much injured in his life, and he had travelled the world over. He wished to address the Bench, but was not allowed to do so ...

The court broke up. One wonders what passed, behind closed doors, between the three Magistrates, de Schmid and Toby. The prisoners were set free, and the crowd streamed out on to Honiton high street. 'As Dowell walked up the street many persons followed him, he, at the same time, protesting his innocence.'

CHAPTER TWELVE

The Inquest Winds Up

Lord Sidmouth, though not chairman of the bench, clearly had no difficulty in persuading his colleagues to dismiss the case. They must have thought its weaknesses too glaring to justify holding the accused any longer, and that Toby would be unable to strengthen it by cross-examining the defence witnesses. However, Colonel Graves's judgment that the evidence did not connect the prisoners with the shooting was ambiguous. He simply meant that the evidence was insufficient to commit the prisoners for trial, not that they were innocent. This was unfortunate, for had the defence case been put, the three accused might have been exonerated and much heartache avoided. Lord Sidmouth's off-hand tone suggests that the bench had little inclination to spend more time on a case involving only labouring people, where the assailant was either a rascally poacher or someone involved in an unsavoury village feud. Dowell himself, while pleased to be able to say in his pamphlet that 'Lord Sidmouth said that it never ought to have been brought before them', was upset that he had not been allowed to clear his name.

But though the criminal hearing was over, the inquest still continued. The Coroner's main concern, in trying to establish the cause of death, was whether the shooting was accidental or intentional. To bring the jury to a sensible decision, he needed Every to put the case for the accused, to see whether or not they could establish alibis. The Coroner had therefore issued a summons for Dowell, Eliza Williams and French to attend.

The villagers, although many had cheered the outcome of the hearing in Honiton, were still no wiser about Perryman's death, and when the third session of the inquest opened in the village schoolroom at 11 a.m. on Monday 1 October, the room was again

TIMEKEEPING

It is worth remembering that, for ordinary people, minute-by-minute precision was difficult. People did not have wrist-watches, and out of doors they mostly told the time by the sun, church bells or predictable comings and goings. Some of the better-off men might have a fob-watch. Surprisingly, since he was poor, John Perryman also had one, which stopped when he was shot. Robert Loveridge said that he 'was particular to see that it kept good time', [1] so it was probably a prized possession, perhaps presented to him for his work as Sunday school superintendent. It seems unlikely, from the way they described their movements on the night of the shooting, that either Bill Dowell or Amos French had a watch.

Inside many houses or public places, there would have been a mantelpiece or wall clock. As we shall see, Agnes Ward, the Perryman's neighbour at Grapevine, heard running footsteps and glanced at the clock (see Appendix D). We may suppose that Eliza, when she specified that she and her brother had been in the Fountain Head 'for half-an-hour and three minutes' had looked at the inn clock as they arrived and left. And we know, from Mrs Northcott's evidence, that when Eliza visited her on the night of the shooting, 'She left, by her timepiece, at 10 minutes to eight o'clock; but the proper time was half-past seven o'clock'. Mrs Northcott must have been referring to a timepiece in her own house, since she knew its vagaries.

More often time was somewhat fluid. Young Jemima French said:

> ... It was after half-past eight o'clock when her father came into the house ... It might have been after nine o'clock when her father was in his house for aught she knew. She had no means of judging the time. [2]

full of eager villagers, who seemed to take a great interest in the proceedings'. [3]

First of all, the Coroner asked the accused to stand forward one by one and give their accounts. We shall treat these as alibis, more or less plausible and persuasive, but also as offering a rare glimpse of village life, the comings and goings, activities and conversations along the small stretch of road between The Fountain Head inn and the Church.

Eliza William'ss story

First to be called was Eliza Williams. The Coroner said 'she could give evidence if she wished for the purpose of clearing herself, and it would be right for her to do so'. She said she wished to, and her account goes as follows.

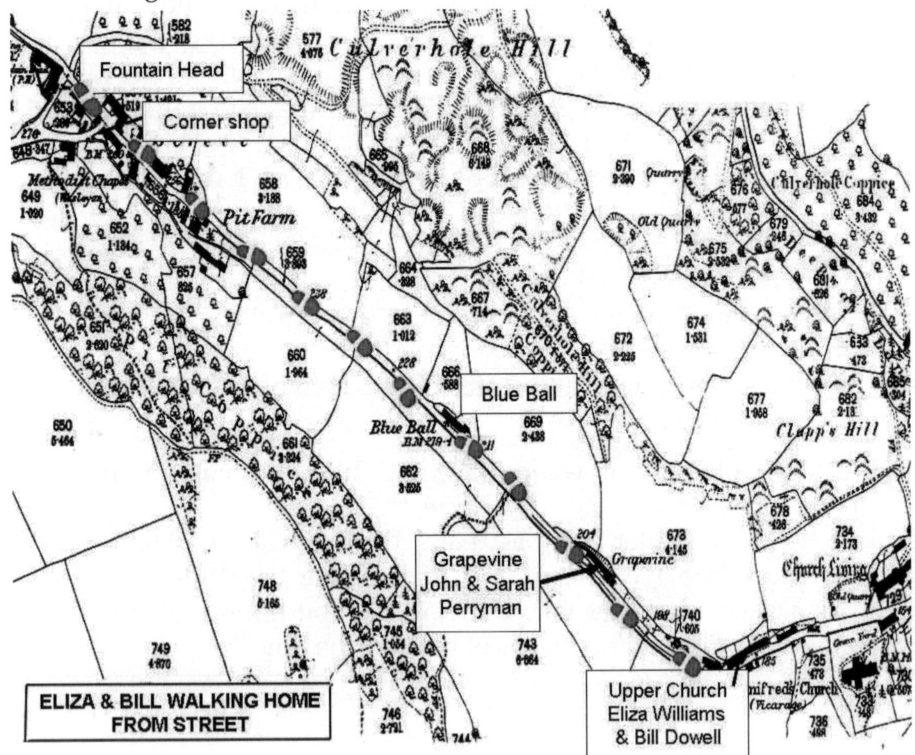

After coming from Honiton in Isaac French's cart (Plate 10) — probably by the turnpike over Farway Common and Broad Down, then by Branscombe Cross and Bulstone to Street — they reached The Fountain Head at about ten past six (so ten past seven, BST). They spent half an hour and three minutes there, talking, and Bill probably had a drink. Although Eliza did not mention it, we know that Bill was 'walking out' with Susan Ann Gill, the innkeeper's sister, a good reason for stopping off to recount the day's happenings. Bill did not want to come home immediately, but Eliza 'pressed him very much to do so, to have some tea'. No doubt she was anxious to get back to her three young children, who were probably being looked after by Mrs Northcott.

They started walking down the road. The weather was dry, so the rough road was dusty. [4] It was beginning to get dark as they passed the rows of cottages below the pub, including, on the opposite side of the road, the once fine house at Margels, now rented out. They passed the corner shop, [5] the Chapel in which John Perryman held Sunday School, and another row of cottages opposite.

Today Street is still a small cluster of cottages and in winter time no more than 20 people live there. In the 1881 Census there were 28 households and 118 people, [6] but at six forty-five in the evening, when Eliza and Bill walked home, it was probably relatively quiet. Most of the men were still out working in the fields, and as the light faded, the women making lace would have set their work aside and begun to busy themselves indoors with the children and getting the tea. [7]

They walked on, past Pitt Farm, past Blue Ball, where Thomas Ward had a small front-room shop, [8] past the long field where the new Chapel would later be built, and past Grapevine with its six households — the two Perryman families, two Ward families and two single women. In part of Collick's Cottage, on the bend below Grapevine, lived Samuel Parrett, boot and shoe maker, and his wife Julianna, a childless couple in their fifties. Passing the entrance to Collick's allotment field, they reached the six cottages of Upper Church. First came the house where John and Sarah Ann Northcott lived with their son and mother-in-law, and then the Raffell family. [9] Finally they turned in at their own front door. According to Eliza, the walk had taken them just seven minutes. (It took us ten, but they walked everywhere and were very fit. We are also older.)

The time was now about ten to seven. Normally there would have been a fire burning in the grate, but because they had been away most of the day it had not been lit and Bill did not settle. Eliza said that when she went upstairs to change her dress,

> he took a jug from the table for the purpose of returning it to Mrs Fred. Williams, from whom it had been borrowed. She lived the next door above. [10]

He came indoors again, hung around for about quarter of an hour, and then went to Mrs Northcott's. He stayed about ten minutes, came back to his own house for five, and went out again. About half an hour later, Eliza saw him come out of Mrs Northcott's house again. He went off, but she did not see where he went. According to Bill's and Eliza's reckonings, it was then about 7.50 pm.

Now it was Eliza's turn to visit Mrs Northcott but she did not stay long. Mrs Northcott, in her evidence, thought that Bill's and Eliza's visits were each between fifteen and thirty minutes, and that Eliza left 'at 10 minutes to eight o'clock; but the proper time was half-past seven o'clock'. This does not quite fit with Eliza's reckoning. But either way, she left the Northcotts between 7.30 and 8.20, a good half-hour or more before Perryman was shot.

Dowell takes the stand

Bill Dowell's story picked up where Eliza's left off. He left Mrs. Northcott, loitered outside his own door for about five minutes, and then went down the road, past David Pile's house and the Wyatts to his friends the Frenches in the end cottage. Mrs French and her daughter Jemima were on their own. Dowell said:

> I talked and joked, and picked up a book which I saw lying on the table. While seated there Amos French came to the

house, and said, "Well, old man, how be 'ee getting on?" I replied, "I believe that pig's tail is the end 'o pork." [11]

Bill mentions that the book on the table was a medical one and that Amos French had given it to him at Honiton — so presumably they had met in town earlier that day. He read on for another quarter of an hour and then went home, having a joke with Jemima on the way out. By Bill's reckoning this should take us to about 8.10 (or by Mrs Northcott's about 7.50).

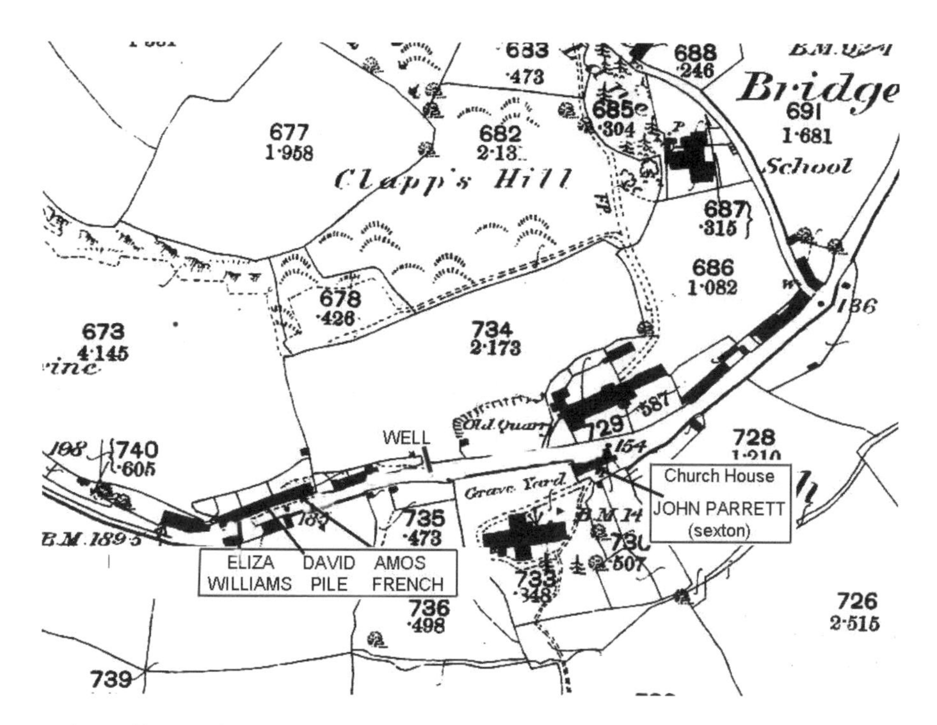

As Bill stood at his own door again Bessie Raffell went by. She was a young woman of twenty-two, but not one of the Raffell family next door. 'Where are you going, old gal?' he asked, and she replied that she was 'going down to the mill, to my work'. [12] He asked her whether he should go with her, and she consented. Bill walked with her as far as the Church, a hundred yards away ('a couple of gunshots', he said — an unfortunate turn of phrase in the middle of an inquest on a shooting!) but then she turned into Church House where John Parrett, the Sexton, lived. Bill waited a couple of minutes but as she did not come out he walked back to Amos French's house. Five minutes later, French came in and sat down, but after three or four minutes he went to get water from the well [13] and Bill left the house with him and went home. By Bill's reckoning, it was now between 8.20 and 8.30.

John Selly, 'a cattle dealer's son', said he passed by at half-past eight, and 'saw Amos French and Dowell in French's house. Dowell was reading a book and French was sitting in a chair'. However, according to the *Exeter Flying Post*, Selly had told the Magistrates' hearing that it was 'about eight o'clock' when he passed by and saw this scene, [14] and this fits better with Bill's account.

A statement of sorts by Amos French

When it came to Amos French's turn to testify, the only report says no more than that

> he gave at some length an account of how he spent his time on the night of the 8th of September, from the moment he arrived home from Honiton up to the time when Perryman was shot. Before nine o'clock he was in his house sitting in a chair asleep.

This remained unchallenged as an alibi for himself, nor was he questioned about Dowell's visits. His daughter Jemima was, but her answer was very vague:

> I could not say at what time he came into my father's house, nor could I swear whether he came in more than once. [15]

By Dowell's reckoning, Amos went out to the well between 8.20 and 8.30, and Jemima added that 'It was after half-past eight o'clock when her father came into the house, and he then went to sleep by the fireside'. But then, Jemima also admitted that 'she had no means of judging the time'. So at a pinch, Amos might have gone to the well, run up Culverwell Hill, shot Perryman at 8.50, and still have pretended to fall asleep beside the fire at nine. An unlikely scenario!

Dowell's alibi?

Bill returned home. Now the exact timing becomes important, and once again Eliza took up the story:

> He went to the linhay for sticks to light the fire, and returned in a few moments. While the water was boiling [he] sat in the house reading a newspaper. I went upstairs to put the children in bed and then I noticed the postman, Mr Searle pass.

Eliza spent about quarter of an hour putting the children to bed, then Bill called up to her, 'The water boils; where is the tea?' She went downstairs; he was still reading the paper, so

> I fetched a frying-pan for him, and he put a piece of meat to fry in it. Just as it was cooked, and my brother was about to "turn it up," I heard someone outside the house speaking to David Pile. I heard them say, "John Perryman is shot." My brother did not say anything, as he was almost too frightened to speak.

For Dowell to have shot John Perryman at 8.50, he would have had to leave his house at 8.40 at the very latest. During this vital period of time, according to what they said, Eliza was upstairs while he was downstairs reading the paper and getting the tea. Eliza said she saw Searle go past, and in evidence given to the previous sitting of the inquest Searle had said he passed the house at twenty to nine. But Searle's evidence was inconclusive, for in one newspaper account he said that he had passed 'But not seeing any light in the window he did not take much notice of the house', [16] and in another, 'When I passed Dowell's and French's cottages, I took no notice, and could not, therefore, say whether anyone was inside. I saw no-one'. Tidwell said much the same: he had gone past the cottages at about twenty to nine 'but could not say whether there were lights inside'. Such cautious statements could neither prove nor disprove an alibi for Dowell nor, for that matter, for French.

After Dowell had finished, Superintendent de Schmid tried to unpick his story: How long had he read the paper for? How long did it take him to fry the meat? Dowell's answers were the same as before — fifteen minutes reading the paper while the water boiled; about five minutes to fry the meat. De Schmid protested that this did not tally with earlier evidence, [17] but the Coroner, very reasonably, pointed out that it was hard to tell the time with accuracy. De Schmid agreed, but still maintained that it was very important. His frustration is understandable. During the crucial twenty minutes when Dowell might have run up through the field behind the house, shot Perryman and run back again, there was only his word and the word of his sister and presumed accomplice for his presence in the house. Even Eliza's statement that she had seen Searle pass by was not necessarily reliable, since she had already heard his evidence that he passed at twenty to nine, and in any case it was Dowell's presence downstairs, not hers upstairs, that was in question.

It is worth pointing out that de Schmid's assumption that anyone could know within ten minutes when someone returning from the harvest field would reach a particular point on his path home is utterly specious, given the long and varying hours worked at that season.[18] And although Dowell and Eliza could not provide a completely watertight alibi, the total effect of their detailed recollections was to build up a picture in which, as the Coroner commented later, 'The conduct of Dowell on the night of the 8th September was not that of a man who was about to commit a serious crime'.

A sceptic and a blabbermouth

The question of the alibi occupied most of the eight hours or so of the third sitting of the inquest, but two other bits of evidence are worth a brief notice.

The Coroner had granted a request from Every for Mr Stamp, the magistrate's clerk at Honiton, to be subpoena'ed to attend. Every (who must have known Stamp well, both being solicitors in

Honiton) made him go over the details of Eliza's and Bill's behaviour in his office on Saturday morning, to establish that they had been satisfied with his suggested remedy for Pile's abuse. Superintendent de Schmid put a crudely leading question: 'Did you not hear Dowell say, when leaving, "I will have it out some other way?"' which Stamp repudiated. His evidence finished with the following exchange:

Stamp: What all this has to do with the death of Perryman, I fail to see.
Every: I quite agree with you.

More entertaining is the testimony relating to Isaac French, the carrier (plate 10). Mr R. Franks, a farmer from Ottery St Mary, alleged that in the Black Lion inn at Honiton on Saturday 15th September, a week after the shooting, he heard French claim that he knew as much about the affair as anyone in Branscombe, that Dowell was in the pub when Perryman was shot, that he would bet £50 that the man who caused his death lived not 150 yards from his own door, and that the shot was intended not for Perryman but for Amos Power.

Here, refreshingly, was an alternative murder theory to that of the police, but unfortunately Isaac French was a hopeless advocate for it. The only one of his assertions that can be checked — that Dowell was in the pub at the time of the shooting — was false. He squirmed miserably under Superintendent de Schmid's questioning, trying to eat his words without perjuring himself. He said he told Amos Power that the shot was meant for him (to which, he said, Power replied 'No one wishes me that harm, do they?') but he could give no reason for having said it. When asked directly 'Do you know who it was that shot Perryman?' he answered 'I do not; and I stand before God and man'. When asked if he was in liquor at the time he held forth in The Black Lion, he replied 'Rather; not over above'. James Farmer, the landlord, agreed that he was not drunk, but added that French 'usually had a good deal to say ... His tongue was always running'. At the end of the inquest the Coroner dismissed all his allegations and said he ought to be ashamed of himself.

Amos Power was the farmer at Elverway. (Dowell, it will be recalled, had suggested to P. C. Martin that Power's sons might be out shooting on the Saturday night that Perryman was shot.) His mild reply to French suggests that he was unlikely to be the intended victim. The only connection seems to be that he rented Culverwell Hill, so an enemy might possibly have expected to find him there. As for who the supposed enemy was, Isaac French lived a few houses below his nephew Amos French, and a circle of 150 yards from his front door encompassed most of the houses around the church.

At eight o'clock, as the light of suspended oil-lamps began to outshine the dusk in the schoolroom, the inquest was adjourned for yet another week. De Schmid, realising that his case was irretrievably lost, was conspicuously absent from the fourth and final sitting, and P. C. Martin was left to carry the can.

The shoemaker's gun

By the time Coroner Cox opened the fourth sitting of his inquest on Monday 8th October much of the excitement had gone out of the proceedings. The Reverend Swansborough sat through, but Henry Ford and John Pyle did not bother to turn up. The Coroner, expecting Superintendent de Schmid to be there to extract further evidence from Martin, looked around and asked

> 'Is there anyone representing the police today, with the exception of Police Constable Martin?'[19]

'No, Sir' replied Martin, and when he took the stand, no doubt feeling abandoned and unhappy, the Coroner led the questioning and Every cross-examined.

Martin again produced his exhibits: the shotgun found in the linhay, the powder, shot and caps found there with it, the shot found in Perryman's bag, and something new: a gun-wad found at the murder scene since the last session of the inquest by P. C. James Moore, the Beer policeman.

Both wad and gun were minutely examined by the jury, some of whom expressed doubts as to the wad fitting the barrel. The wad was not of the ordinary description but apparently composed of leather. [20] The stock of the gun was bound around with a "wax-end" used by shoemakers.

However, a vital piece of evidence was missing and the villagers expressed their disapproval:

Martin: When I found the gun in question there was an exploded cap on it. I am of opinion that the gun had been recently discharged, but I have lost the exploded cap. (*Hisses.*)

Coroner: How is it you lost the cap?

Martin: I don't know; I put it away somewhere and can't find it. (*Hisses.*)

Coroner: Someone appears to be making a noise which is not generally allowed in a Coroner's Court. If that occurs again I shall have the disturber excluded from the room.

Martin: I removed the cap from the gun and put it away, but where I put it I cannot say. I should think that the gun had been discharged [within] two or three weeks, as the nipple was quite fresh.

Martin was in a parlous situation. He had to try to maintain that the gun had been fired recently, while pretending to have lost the give-away evidence that it had not, yet without exposing either himself or de Schmid to accusations of perjury. He was clearly floundering, and now Every weighed in:

Every: Did you not tell me at Honiton that you had that cap at home?

Martin: I said I believed it was at home.

Every: Do you know that a discharged cap is one of the greatest tests one can have as to whether a gun has been discharged?

Martin: It all depends upon where it is kept.

Every: Did you not say that cap had verdigris on it?

Martin: No.
Every: Did not the superintendent of police say so?
Martin: He did.
Every: Did he not say that he wouldn't swear that the gun had not been discharged for a month?
Martin: He did.
Every: I understand you to say that you will not swear that the gun had been discharged within a month of the time you found it? [21]
Martin: I will not, but I think it had.

Now Every turned to the leather gun-wad. This was a critical issue, for he had subpoena'ed Henry Saunders Parrett, the owner of the gun, to come and give in person the evidence disallowed by the magistrates at Honiton — evidence to the effect that the gun had not been fired in the last two months. But Parrett was a shoemaker; his gun-stock was bound with a shoemaker's wax-end; and now the finding of an unusual gun-wad made of leather might well be damaging, for it suggested that the gun which killed Perryman belonged to a shoemaker. Once again Every turned on Martin:

Every: Was the gun-wad produced at Honiton?
Martin: No, sir.
Every: Is it an ordinary wad?
Martin: Well, you do not often see one like it.
Every: You believe that the wad came from the gun produced?
Martin: I will not swear to that.
Every: You produce it, I suppose, as coming from the gun?
Martin: Not at all.
Every: But simply as a gun-wad found at the spot?
Martin: Yes. It fits the gun.

This was enough to drive a wedge of doubt between the wad and the gun, and when Henry Parrett was called he said the gun, which was his, had been where it was found for two years:

> I'm certain that no one had had the gun unless they had entered my linhay like Martin did, and took it away. However, I saw that no one had been in my linhay, because

> nothing was displaced. I loaded the gun last May to fire it off, but I didn't do so, and returned it to the shelf in the linhay. About five or six weeks before Perryman was shot I fired the gun towards the sea, because I was afraid to leave it longer loaded.

Then came the important detail — and a direct challenge:

> *Parrett:* Martin had told him that there was an old "blue-vinnied" cap on the gun when he found it, and he might have brought it if he had liked. [22]
> *Martin:* How do you know?
> *Parrett:* Well, you told me it was there.

Questioned further, Parrett agreed that Amos French had a linhay near his, but denied that French could see the gun from outside the linhay. Nor could anyone have entered it without unhanging the gate, because it was kept locked. He had been in the linhay since September 8 and 'Nothing was disturbed, not even a potato, and there were no indications of the gate having been unhung'. He had never cut a leather wad. By now Every must have been satisfied that he had scotched the idea that Amos French might have purloined the gun for Dowell's use. The gun from the linhay had become a red herring.

Murdered by persons unknown

The last witness to be called was James Perryman, John's elder brother. Unlike the police, he seems to have believed that his brother's death was probably a poaching accident, and pointed out that there had been shooting on Culverwell Hill earlier that week. He said

> that he was at the Wesleyan Chapel on the 5th of September, and left about 10 minutes past eight o'clock. He arrived home about 20 minutes past eight o'clock. He lived next door to his late brother. While he was proceeding home he heard the report of a gun from the direction of the place where his brother was shot. This was three nights before ...

Now all the evidence had been heard. Every rose and addressed the jury on behalf of William Dean Dowell, Amos French and Eliza Williams. After reminding them of all that they had heard, he launched into his peroration:

> There was nothing before them to link the story of the journey to Honiton with the return of the labourers from Edge Farm on the night of the 8th except suspicion — and suspicion was rank, and had got hold of men in the village.

Then, allowing that 'It was not his province to suggest or to intimate any possible theory as to how this unfortunate crime took place', he proceeded to do just that —

> It was clear, from the evidence of James Perryman, that a man was shooting on Culverwell Hill on the Wednesday before John Perryman was shot. The time was twenty minutes past eight o'clock: and what right, he would ask, had anyone shooting there at that time of night? Anyone lying prone on the spot where the fatal shot was fired would be able to see a rabbit and kill one. It was a possible theory, but he (Mr Every) would not say that it was correct, that a person might have seen a rabbit and shot at it.

Having thus tried to plant the idea of a poaching accident in the jurors' minds, he returned to his main brief, and emphatically declared

> that there had not been one particle, one fragment, or one tittle of evidence against Dowell, Williams, or French ... and no justification on the part of the police for the arrest of anyone.

As he sat down the village audience burst into 'Applause, which was immediately suppressed'.

The Coroner now summed up in detail, and went on to direct the jury, as follows:

> It was quite possible, as Mr Every had suggested, that the affair was an accident, but it was not at all probable. If the death of Perryman was the result of an accident, it was

> difficult to suppose that the person who had caused the death would not come forward in the face of three persons actually having been accused of the murder.

He dealt at length with the behaviour and possible motives of the three accused, and concluded that

> As far as the evidence sworn to, there was not the slightest proof of either of the accused [*i.e.* Dowell or French] having committed the crime ... [and] taking the whole of the evidence into consideration, he could not see the slightest possible evidence to connect any particular person with the cause of the death of Perryman.

The jury, after a few minutes deliberation, returned a verdict of 'Wilful murder against some person or persons unknown', and the Coroner concurred: 'I think that is a perfectly proper verdict, and I entirely agree with you'.

The Coroner had gone much further than the Magistrates by asserting that the three accused had no connection at all with the crime. On the other hand, his unconvincing assumption that if the killing had been accidental the perpetrator's conscience would have driven him to confess, was unfortunate. If he had given equal weight to the possibility of accidental death much of the fear and anger that continued to engulf the village might have been avoided. As it was, it seemed that a murderer was still at large in Branscombe.

PART SIX

VILLAGE IN TURMOIL

CHAPTER THIRTEEN

An Unsatisfactory Outcome

Giving up or covering up?

Was that it? Was it all over? The case had been dismissed by the magistrates, the accused had had their say at the inquest, Every's witnesses had been heard, and the police case was demolished. The jury had agreed unanimously that John Perryman had been murdered, but that the identity of the murderer was unknown. After which the press packed their bags, went home and thought no more about it — with the honourable exception of Richard Lethaby.

One might have thought that in a rural area where people were rarely murdered, responsible people would have wanted to reopen the inquiry. But it seems the Honiton magistrates made no suggestion that a more experienced detective than de Schmid be asked to take over. And two weeks later, when Quarter Sessions was held in Exeter, the case was not even mentioned. Once again, Lethaby, in his Sidmouth paper, was scathing:

> We can believe that if [Sir John Kennaway] or some other magistrates we could name, had had the affair to oversee and investigate, the issue would not have been so unsatisfactory as it now is. It is, however, to be regretted that at the County Quarter Sessions held in Exeter on October 16, when there was an unusually large number of magistrates present, not a word was said about the affair, either by the Chief Constable in his report, or by anyone else. And this though hours were spent in discussing the personal grievance of a Superintendent against the Chief Constable. That may have been correct and proper;

> but some notice might have been taken of this foul blot upon the county's character — a blot which in other parts of the country would have led to its appointed peace guardians to offer a reward, and invoke the aid of the Home Secretary. [1]

Bill Dowell wondered whether the police simply wanted to draw a veil over their incompetence:

> The case itself must have cost the county of Devon hundreds of pounds, the fruits of employing men that do not understand their duty. After we were discharged there, they let the case stop, never so much as offering a reward, and the case was not so much as brought up at the county sessions following … I suppose the Superintendent was ashamed to, after making such a bungling job of it as he did. [2]

It was indeed a curious business. The minutes of the hearing in the Honiton Petty Sessions book read as follows:

> Ref. French)
Dowell) Murder
Williams)
>
> Depositions taken on separate paper — prisoners discharged. [3]

The 'separate paper' has not survived. Was this a case of extreme casualness, or extreme protectiveness by the Honiton magistrates towards their superintendent? Whichever, de Schmid, neither moved nor promoted, continued in charge of the Honiton division until he retired some thirty years later.

The village divided

As far as the outside world was concerned, the matter was closed. However for the villagers, and for the accused, nothing had been resolved. No one knew who had shot John Perryman, and as far as they could tell the culprit still lurked in their midst. People were fearful and upset and divided. The Coroner had opted for wilful murder and plenty of people must have continued to regard the three accused with suspicion. 'No smoke without fire', they would say, and mutter that they had 'got away with murder' only because the police had not been able to prove their guilt. Lethaby was right when he said: 'However innocent they may be of the crime, a stigma must and will attach to them as long as they live'.

Others refused to believe that it was a premeditated killing. Every, for the defence, had suggested that it might have been a poaching accident; John Perryman's brother James implied at the inquest that he thought it likely; and Dowell himself was sure of it.

One can imagine the sullen bitterness that continued to bedevil the village, and the way in which divisions within the community were exacerbated. It was the poorer villagers who had stood outside The Fountain Head, packed the schoolroom, and made their way (mainly on foot) to attend Petty Sessions in Honiton. It was they that had enlivened proceedings by hissing when de Schmid and P. C. Martin failed to produce the shot or the cap; applauded Every's concluding speech in the school-room; cheered the Magistrates' verdict in Honiton and triumphantly followed the acquitted trio up the street afterwards. And it was they who, according to Dowell, immediately offered financial assistance after the inquest:

> After we were discharged and every thing paid, a lot of the poor villagers persuaded us to have a subscription list, and they promised us various sums of money, half-a-crown to one penny. I said no, I would not accept any from the poor people, but the others could please themselves. [4]

But by no means all the poorer people supported him. Gender may have been an important divide. Because the men were working in the fields, it was mainly women who had packed the school-room and court-room, and heard for themselves what the accused had to say in their defence. As Every said in his final speech, 'suspicion was rank, and had got hold of *men* in the village.'

The more important people in the village, or at least the more important men, seem to have favoured the theory of a murder plot rather than a shooting accident. The farmers on the jury took this line, allowing the finger of suspicion to remain pointing at Dowell and his alleged accomplices. Dowell himself was convinced that the squire and the vicar were against him and Eliza. After they had been cleared, he said,

> My sister went down to the vicar of the parish and asked him if he would make her out a paper, he being the "shepherd of the flock," he hesitated, and then said "No, not now, he would go over and see Mr. Ford about it." [5]

There may have been another divide, this time between church and chapel. The small Methodist chapel was mostly attended by people who lived at Street and by labouring families from outlying farms, while most of those who went to St. Winifred's lived near the church or at Vicarage. A few of the better-off families, like the Chicks, were Methodists, but mainly the chapel was filled by poorer villagers. For them the loss of their much-loved Sunday school superintendent, their leader in prayer and song, was a disaster. They could have felt vengeful, but it seems that that was not their way. Following the lead of James Perryman, they appear for the most part to have believed that his brother's death was an accident, and when it came to inscribing his gravestone, they said as much.

In contrast, although the Dowells, Williamses and Frenches were church-going families, it seems probable that, under the influence of the Reverend Swansborough and Squire Ford, the church-goers remained more apt to believe the story of 'wilful murder'. Even the sparse interventions at the inquest by jurymen are suggestive in this regard. The farmer William Pike, who twice queried David Pile's testimony in an aggressive manner, implying that he was lying to protect the accused, was a crony of Henry Ford's, and became churchwarden, along with Henry Ford, in 1884. On the other hand, John Collins, who quibbled over Perryman's last words, as if to leave open the possibility that, in so far as Perryman himself witnessed it, the shooting was accidental, was a bootmaker's kit-maker from Street, and a Methodist.

So the proceedings laid nothing to rest, and as Agnes Ward, a small girl at the time of the shooting, later said to her great-nephew Bill Carpenter, 'a very bad atmosphere prevailed in the village' (Appendix D).

Dowell attempts to find the assailant

Bill Dowell was so shaken by the injustice of it all, and by the way some of the village people treated him, that he decided to emigrate to Australia. But for the time being he stayed on, desperate to clear his name, and convinced that the killing was an accident. He did not blame a poacher for taking a gun out, but he certainly blamed him for not coming forward, and used his pamphlet to make a direct appeal:

> I pray and beseech you, man of Branscombe, to come forward and confess it. If you were up there on the Culverwell Hills to shoot a rabbit for your wife and children's Sunday dinner, I commend you for it, for I know the few shillings per week you get for your labour, will not allow you to buy much meat ... But when you found you had shot a man, you ought to have gone to his assistance, and stated the truth, instead of running away and leaving him to die. Then every man in the parish, with a spark of human feeling in his breast would have pitied you.

He reassured the person involved that, according to a 'London man of law',

> If the party was to come forward now and prove that it was an accident, which every right-thinking man can see it was, he would get punished, but only very little: that would be for not coming forward when innocent persons were charged with it.[6]

He offered a reward. He would do anything to help the man, if he would only own up:

> If the party that fired the fatal shot will only come forward and confess to it before I leave this country I will forgive him freely for all I have suffered and am suffering now. I will be

> his friend through life, and my two brothers [7] and myself in London will give him £50 and whatever he has to pay or suffer through confessing to it.

But still no one admitted to the shooting.

CHAPTER FOURTEEN

Illicit Liaisons, Illegitimate Children

Two surprises

Any village, in an age before contraception, had its fair share of illegitimate births. Branscombe parish registers indicate that more often than not a man married his woman after she had become pregnant. Apart from anything else, he then knew she was fertile. On other occasions, when a woman found herself pregnant and could not marry, her parents took on the child and pretended it was theirs. Or, third possibility, an illegitimate baby was acknowledged as such and mother and child usually continued to live with the mother's parents. When an illegitimate baby was baptised, the Reverend Swansborough, unlike his predecessors, wrote 'Base' in the margin of the register and sometimes noted down the name of the father. In these cases the man probably acknowledged paternity, and perhaps paid something towards maintenance. But if such informal arrangements broke down, the father might be sued in the magistrates' court at Honiton and made to pay up. It is not clear how illegitimate children were regarded, but it seems likely that they sometimes had a hard time of it.

What has all this to do with the aftermath of the shooting? In the months that followed, when feelings were volatile and ran high, it seems there may have been more than the usual amount of extra-marital sex. We cannot easily substantiate this from the baptism registers because, although sex usually led to pregnancy, by no means all children were baptised. Nevertheless, in the five months between September 1884 and February 1885 four illegitimate births were registered, compared with none in the four and a half years between February 1880 and September 1884. Before that the rate had been slightly less than one a year: fifteen in the sixteen years between 1864 and 1880.

In August 1884 Bessie Raffell (whom Bill Dowell escorted down the road on the evening of the shooting) had a daughter, Lottie Helena, by John Gill; [1] In December 1884 Thereza Anna Quick had a son by one of the Wards; and — here comes the first shock — William Dean Dowell fathered a child by Susan Ann Gill! Their daughter, Flossie Alice, was born on 22 December 1884:

1885	1885. January 25. No 222	Flossie Alice born 22nd Decr	(Father William Dean Dowell) Susan Ann	Gill	Fountain Head	Single Woman	R Swansborough Vicar
Base.							

And — second shock — Eliza Williams, whose husband Thomas was still in the asylum, gave birth to a baby daughter, Ellen, on 22 February 1885:

Base.	1885. July 25. No. 253	Ellen born 22nd Feby 1885.	Eliza	Williams	Church	Husband (Thomas) a Labourer for several years past in the Asylum at Exminster	R Swansborough Vicar

Working back from these dates, Susan Ann Gill conceived Flossie in late March 1884, some five months after the inquest ended, and Eliza conceived Ellen two months later, in late May 1884. [2]

'My girl'

For us, who had spent so long poring over Bill Dowell's pamphlet, these discoveries came as a big surprise. True, Dowell had dropped a mention of a woman friend, but very much in passing. He said that on the Sunday evening after the shooting, he left the Masons Arms because he 'had to go and see my girl.' [3] He did not name her, and it was only when we found out about the baby that we realised that 'my girl' was the Miss Gill who, as P. C. Martin told the inquest, walked down the road from the Fountain Head to Eliza Williams's house with him and Dowell on the following Monday.

Who was Susan Ann Gill? She belonged to an extensive Gill clan, most of whose menfolk were carpenters, and who in a previous generation had been smuggling partners with Matthew Williams. Her father John Gill (1822-1911) had married Mary Ann Clarke in July 1848 and Susan Ann was born in September of the same year. She had one sister and five surviving brothers, all carpenters. At the time of the shooting her father was a widower, who lived and had his workshop at 'Yew Tree', a house in Street belonging to Henry Ford. Susan Ann and two of her brothers, Thomas and George, lived opposite, at The Fountain Head (plate 9). Thomas was innkeeper, and according to the 1881 census she acted as 'housekeeper'. The male Gills were not much given to matrimony; only two of Susan Ann's five brothers ever married, and of those, George was quickly widowed and never remarried. Susan Ann herself was thirty-five, the same age as Eliza, when she and Bill Dowell were 'walking out' in 1883. He was thirty-one.

Dowell presumably did not want to complicate his narrative with 'irrelevant' information, but could not resist a small allusion easily understood by anyone in the village who read his pamphlet. But, of course, once we discover that he had fathered a child, it changes our understanding of what was going on in the period after the acquittal. By March, if not before, he and Susan Ann had become lovers. It seems they had not hidden their relationship, and it is likely they hoped to get married, all the more urgently once they realised that she was pregnant.

But they did not marry. The story that has come down through Flossie's family is that they were very much in love but were not allowed to marry. [4] If so, since there seems no obvious reason why Dowell's family should object, we must suppose that the Gills were against it. Presumably they were hostile not because Bill got her pregnant but because they still regarded him with suspicion. So Bill's desperation to clear his name was not only a question of honour, but also due to the fact that he could not marry Susan Ann until he had done so.

Plate 9. The Fountain Head at Street with the Gills

Plate 10. Isaac French with his van

Plate 11. 1897 - the Miss Adlams' class with Ellen Williams

Plate 12. Methodist meeting with Eliza Williams

Dowell says that he stayed in the village until September 1884. [5] He left, therefore, in the sixth month of Susan Ann's pregnancy, and missed the birth of his baby daughter. Why did he leave? He probably needed to earn money. But, more importantly, he may have found that since he had been unable to clear his name in the intervening months, the Gill family remained obstinately opposed to his making an honest woman of Susan Ann. There may have been some critical event of which we know nothing, and Susan Ann herself may have turned against him, for it seems he did not offer to help with child maintenance. In February 1885 she brought a paternity suit against him in Honiton, which was uncontested, and Captain Graves ordered him to pay 2s 6d per week for sixteen years towards the keep of his child. [6]

Father unknown?

By the time Bill left the village in September 1884 his sister Eliza was more than four months pregnant. Her husband, as everyone knew, and as the Reverend Swansborough unnecessarily noted in the baptismal register, was in Exminster asylum. And although the baby Ellen, being the daughter of a married woman, could have been treated as legitimate, Swansborough still wrote 'Base' in the margin. He did not write down the father's name, and the little girl's paternity seems to have remained a well-kept secret.

A possible candidate, of course, is Eliza's neighbour Amos French. Their affectionate relationship had already aroused David Pile's jealousy, and the ordeal of imprisonment, trial and inquest, could have brought them even closer together. In the turbulent months that followed they may have briefly become lovers. But this is no more than surmise, and the two families continued to live close to each other for many years at Upper Church.

Eliza's position must have become extremely difficult. Her brother had left under a cloud, and the Williams family record of mental instability may have added to her isolation. We do not know why her brother-in-law (and landlord) William Williams cut his throat in November 1886, but one can well imagine that the family appeared to be under some hereditary curse, just as some people explained all Dowell's misfortunes by his defiance of the wizard Cross. One way or another, the scandals swirling around the Dowell and Williams families can only have exacerbated bad feelings towards them in the village.

CHAPTER FIFTEEN

Political Awakening

Conservatism under threat

All this might seem reason enough for Dowell to think about emigrating to Australia. But there were also political reasons for the village to be stirred up, and to be stirred up against him.

Dowell said that before he moved to the Midlands in the 1870s, his 'views up to that time had been Conservative' — that is, he had been raised in the unthinking conservatism, both small 'c' and big, woven into the social fabric of rural East Devon. Right through to 1884, 'views' were all that most people in Branscombe could have, for only the few owners of freehold property were entitled to vote in parliamentary elections. But in 1884 Gladstone's Liberal government brought in the Third Reform Act which gave the vote to male householders in the counties, adding at a stroke some six million men to the electorate. The two parties squared up for an election in 1885, in which the Liberals hoped to challenge the Tories' traditional rural dominance.

The promise of the vote gave a new edge to the latent grievances of agricultural workers, and occasions were reported in East Devon when angry or drunken men torched hayricks or set fire to the thatch of a hated farmer. [1] The evidence from Branscombe on this point is equivocal. Tony Hibbert claims that Berry Barton and four other farms were burnt down by disaffected farm workers in 1875. [2] Two possible candidates for Hibbert's list would be Cotte Barton and Cox's Farm, but the former seems to have been destroyed in the 1840s [3] and the latter in the late 1860s. According to Elijah Chick, Berry Barton was burnt somewhat later, on 27 September 1887. [4]

For despite farm-workers' grievances, Branscombe remained deeply conservative. Just how Conservative it was politically can be gauged from a surviving copy of the Branscombe electoral roll for 1885, annotated by hand with people's voting intentions. [5] Conservatives were marked 'C', others either 'R' or 'D'. 'R' must stand for Radical, and denotes those intending to vote Liberal. [6] 'D' probably stands for 'Declined' (to say) and these too were likely to vote Liberal. Out of 159 registered voters (not counting those marked absent, dead, at sea, etc.) 136 (85.5%) are marked 'C', 11 (6.9%) 'R', and 12 (7.5%) 'D'.

If we treat the 23 R+D's as the potential Liberal vote in the village, they comprised 6 artisans (a stonemason, baker, tailor, thatcher and two shoemakers) a fisherman and a gardener, and 15 farm-workers. They include some who have featured in our story — David Pile, John Northcott, Thomas Newton, James Searle, Samuel Coombs, James Gosling, and Henry Saunders Parrett. Some working-class voters, therefore, were already drawn to the Liberals, although many more were ready to vote Conservative out of traditional habits of deference. As Harry Hansford put it, 'If you put a blue bow on your pussy-cat, it'd be elected for parliament!' [7]

Of course, how people said they would vote was not always how they actually voted. Farm labourers knew they risked losing their jobs if they admitted to voting Liberal. Even in the twentieth century a man could be in trouble. Laura Somers told a story:

> Father rented cliff plots from Pike of Berry farm and helped on the farm at haymaking and harvesting. He was a proper old Liberal, used to think the farmers were down on the working class. At election time Harry Pike saw George wearing a yellow ribbon, and said, "I'll never give George Dowell another day's work." [And he didn't, and George Dowell took up road-mending for the next twenty-five years.] [8]

Phoebe Spencer added: 'Mrs Leonard, the butcher, used to put Conservative posters in the shop window, and then vote Liberal'. And Les Collier put it more generally:

> You kicked one dog, you kicked the whole lot. The [people in the big houses] were all connected and you had to walk the straight and narrow. No such things as trade unions — you either took what they offered or walked off down the road.

Clearly it was wiser to keep your voting intentions to yourself.

What gave some villagers the courage to be open about their Liberal leanings was Methodism. Nonconformists formed the backbone of Liberal support in the country as a whole, and the connection also shows up in Branscombe. Of the 23 R+D's, 10 appear as fathers in the Methodist baptism register, and a few more who were unmarried or childless were also probably Methodists. On the other hand, only 6 of those named as fathers in the Methodist baptism register are marked 'C' on the electoral roll (details in Appendix C).

This, then, was the climate of political opinion in Branscombe in 1884, when Bill Dowell was hanging around the village and airing the radical opinions that later appeared in his pamphlet. We have only indirect evidence on how the political tensions surrounding this first democratic election fed into the already turbulent atmosphere, and much of it comes from 1885, when Dowell had left. But it throws retrospective light on what he had to put up with.

Battle is joined

Now that working men had the vote and Liberal candidates were putting the case for reform to village audiences, a slow political awakening began in the countryside, and the Tory establishment recognised the need to organise at grass-roots level.

Henry Ford was the chief instigator in Branscombe. From 1882 he and J. A. Orchard, the local Conservative agent, met annually in Sidmouth for a 'necessary revision of the Branscombe list of voters' [9] and by February 1884 a Branscombe Conservative Committee had been formed. [10] In the same year Henry Ford represented Branscombe at a meeting of the East Devon Conservative

Association in Exeter to study the effects of the redistribution of seats.[11]

Throughout 1884 the political temperature rose, and in October a huge demonstration in support of the Reform Bill was held in Exeter with contingents arriving from all over the county. On 16 October the Liberal candidate for East Devon tried to address the Sidmouth and District Liberal Association, but the meeting was disrupted by Tory hecklers and rowdies. Richard Lethaby, trying to propose a motion in support of the Bill, was 'frequently interrupted'. Here is an excerpt from his newspaper account:[12]

There was a crowded attendance, but many persons were deterred from going because of rumours that there would be opposition and uproar. At the appointed time the gentlemen announced, together with Mr. Perry, the Secretary of the East Devon Liberal Association, and several local supporters, ascended the platform, and the proceedings commenced. Says the Exeter newspaper, in its report, —"In the course of the meeting a fight ensued, and walking sticks, apples, nuts, and plaster from the walls were flung about. At the close of the meeting it was only with difficulty that the room was cleared." To the truth of this statement we can personally testify, having been hit on the side of the face by a large piece of apple.

Orchard, the Conservative agent, was a leading interrupter, greeted by Liberal hisses and cries of 'Turn him out', but there were many others, and Lethaby claimed that 'We could give the names of a score of men who were active abettors of the uproar'. In December he published a letter from 'Verax':

> I have lived in Sidmouth but a short time; sufficiently long however to convince me that morally speaking, it is the most God-forsaken place in the kingdom ... To be a Liberal here is

> to subject oneself to petty persecutions on every hand. So strong is the spirit of intolerance, that for Liberals to meet together for any purpose is to invite insult and molestation ... they say that the disturbance of the meeting was designed as a punishment for their daring to hold a meeting in a Tory stronghold ... That the Tories are strong here in numbers I admit; but it is only the savage that uses his strength to batter out the life of his foe.[13]

Even in Branscombe, attempts to hold Liberal meetings met with stiff resistance (see next page) and someone with Dowell's opinions would have been very much *persona non grata*. When he left in the autumn of 1884, local Conservatives would have been heartily relieved to see the back of him, and when, only a few months later, his pamphlet began to circulate, they would have been outraged. Henry Ford was worried enough at the Radical propaganda coming into the village, without the addition of Dowell's polemic. In May 1885 he wrote to Sir John Kennaway M.P. urgently requesting more Conservative leaflets:

> I have called a meeting for Monday next here ... We are not leaving a stone unturned. Our opponents are all very busy. I hear that leaflets and pamphlets are being distributed by the bearers of the weekly Radical papers which find their way into almost every cottager's house.[14]

Here is a sample of Dowell's rhetoric:[15]

> What would it be for the man that owns the whole village to build a reading room and supply it with papers and books. No, that is against their creed, they wish to keep them in ignorance, especially now the Franchise Bill is passed for the poor labourer, which gives him the right to vote the same as the rich for Members of Parliament. Men of Branscombe, vote for the party that will alter the landlaws, and give to you part of the fruits of your labour, you have gained money enough for other people, your childern have gone with hungry bellies long enough, while you have put hundreds of pounds in the bank for others. Beware of the party that preaches what they do not practice.

ILL-RECEIVED LIBERAL SPEECHES IN BRANSCOMBE

In May 1885 the Liberal candidate spoke in Branscombe schoolroom and boldly promised that 'the severance of the labourer from the land must be remedied by a compulsory taking of the land' which would then 'be more distributed'. Henry Ford and the Rev. Swansborough frequently interrupted, and a hand-written account in the Ford papers conveys the flavour of the event — Swansborough pouring scorn on the candidate who, thoroughly unnerved, gave feebler and feebler answers:

'*Swansborough* : What do you mean by the compulsory taking of the land from those to whom it belongs, for the supposed benefit of the labourer?

'*Candidate*: In using the term compulsory I am alluding to only the land taken for railways.

'This statement was promptly and warmly denied by the Vicar, who was upheld by the meeting. All the candidate could say was that he regretted he had not made his meaning more plain, but the land should be in the hands of those who ought to have it. Further asked by the Vicar who ought to have it, and who had any better claim than the possessor, whose money or that of his forefathers had bought it, he said the question did not fairly arise out of what he had said, and he thought the land should be in the hands of those who ought to have it.'

A second Liberal harangue in Branscombe by a Mr Howes of Leeds, was described in a heavily satirical article in the *Devon and Exeter Daily Gazette*, a Tory paper. Henry Ford marked his copy 'Not to be destroyed', and he may well have been the author. Part of the opening paragraph will suffice:

'One element in the proceedings was instructive, and worth remembering as an axiom —*To ensure applause at the right moment, and inspire that unanimity which will go down with others at a distance as agreement of the audience with the sentiments expressed, be sure to bring with you to an open-air meeting a waggon-load of your sympathisers.'*

Most of the villagers present, it was claimed, were women and children, and many more were farm lads, none of them eligible to vote.[16]

Writing his account of what had happened to him, mixed with these heady political declamations, Dowell grew convinced that 'they' — the village establishment — had had a hand in his arrest the year before, and that they would have been glad to have seen him put away or even hanged. His suspicions may have been justified, although we have found nothing to substantiate his claim. Or it may be that his feeling of being scapegoated by the Tory farmers was something that developed in the months spent in the village after the trauma of trial and inquest when the febrile political atmosphere became part of the toxic mix of animus against him and his associates.

CHAPTER SIXTEEN

Burnt in Effigy

Bill Dowell left in September 1884, and a couple of months later, those who for their many different reasons hated him and Eliza Williams and Amos French burned them in effigy.

We would never have known about this startling event if Agnes Ward had not talked in her old age to her great-nephew Bill Carpenter (Appendix D). She was a child of nine when it happened, but remembered that 'a very bad atmosphere prevailed in the village'. Then, almost casually, she added: 'They burnt Bill Dowell, Eliza Williams and Amos French in effigy on the cliff-top'.

EFFIGY BURNING IN DEVON

It was not uncommon for effigies other than Guy Fawkes to be burnt on Bonfire Night. In nineteenth-century Devon effigies were burnt to settle scores or to pillory unpopular local figures.[1] Effigies of the Vicar of Colyton and his curate were burnt in 1866 for imposing high church ritual on a low-church town.[2] A year later, the effigy of a turnpike keeper who had informed on two Branscombe smugglers was paraded through Sidbury, Salcombe Regis and Branscombe and then burnt. On November 5th 1871 an effigy was burnt in Honiton, after being carried in a procession with 'a proclamation concerning it made in a loud voice'. Also on the same night in Exeter an 'official of the city, who is supposed to have been putting on the screw in some fiscal matters was burnt in effigy'.[3]

She gave no date, but it must have happened in 1884 [4] and we are pretty sure it was on November the fifth. Throughout the county Guy Fawkes Night was a time for getting drunk, for masking and revenge, fire-balls and house-burning. According to Dowell, it was on Guy Fawkes Night in 1871 that the effigy of the Reverend Tomkins was paraded through Branscombe and then burnt, 'surplice, bible and all', outside his vicarage. Tomkins too had run foul of Henry Ford and the farmers composing the Vestry, and shortly after the effigy-burning he left the village. Now it was the turn of Dowell, Eliza and Amos French.

Why did this happen in November 1884 rather than November 1883, straight after the conclusion of the Perryman case? We suspect that people got swept up in this display of communal anger and mistrust for different and perhaps conflicting reasons, some old, some new. Some people still harboured the same old suspicions surrounding Perryman's death, for nothing had been resolved and the three accused were still seen as the potential villains. For Tory loyalists, Dowell deserved to be pilloried for his Liberal harangues, and warned never to come back. There may even have been a semi-superstitious fear of Dowell and his sister — he had dared to thwart the wizard, she was connected with too many mentally afflicted people. But most important, perhaps, and most recent, was a sense of outrage at the perceived sexual misdemeanours of the three. Bill had got a woman pregnant, and, for whatever reasons — gossip-mongers would have supplied plenty, real and imaginary — he had abandoned her. Eliza's pregnancy was now obvious, and gossip about who the father could be, picking over the details of the quarrel with David Pile which had come out at the inquest and trial, may well have fixed on Amos French.

We know from Flora Thompson's *Larkrise to Candleford*, an account of life in the small hamlet of Juniper Hill in Oxfordshire in the 1880s, that while pregnant brides were tolerated, adultery was not. Adultery was a breach of the Seventh Commandment and threatened the emotional and economic stability of family and community life. According to Thompson, the village people detested 'loose living' and in a rare case of adultery they found a traditional way to punish and humiliate the sinners:

> The guilty couple had been treated to 'rough music'. Effigies of the pair had been made and carried aloft on poles by torchlight to the house of the woman, to the accompaniment of the banging of pots, pans, and coal-shovels, the screeching of tin whistles and mouth-organs, and cat-calls, hoots and jeers. [5]

This is a scaled-down version of 'skimmington riding', a popular demonstration once practised all over the country by which communities shamed and ridiculed loose-living or husband-beating wives, and more rarely wife-beating husbands. [6] There was probably an element of skimmington in the treatment meted out to the 'adulterers' at Upper Church.

Although there were reasons enough for retribution to be in the air, the effigy burning must have been the result of discussion and planning. It was the sort of thing that was probably drunkenly mooted and decided one night in a pub, and at The Fountain Head Thomas Gill might even have encouraged such talk. We know that the younger Gill brothers were drinkers — two of them had been up before the magistrates on 31 October 1883 for drunken brawling in their own brother's pub. [7] Old John Gill, still head of the family, had the reputation of a hard man, and the Gills had their reasons for wanting to see Bill Dowell disgraced. If it was they who had prevented him from marrying Susan Ann, it must have been because they still suspected him of the murder; if not, they would have wanted to avenge his desertion. They were staunch Tories [8] and Dowell had come to represent everything that they disliked. As carpenters, they could easily lay their hands on what was needed to make effigies and the poles to carry them.

One can well imagine a riotous crowd gathering at Street on November 5th 1884, drinking their fill, and then setting off down the village road. Along the way, people hearing the noise would have run out to join them. How soon would it have been before those in Upper Church realised what was happening? And how terrifying for Eliza and Amos and their families when they did! Effigies being flaunted outside their houses, hideous noise, jeering and abuse. Fear that their roofs might be set on fire. And then, if they dared to look out, seeing the torch-lit procession winding through the churchyard and up to the cliff-top beyond. Seeing the flames beginning to leap up into the night sky, hearing the shouts reverberate across the valley — a desperate moment.

Dowell had, of course, left for London, but the news would have come through soon enough. What could it have felt like? Not surprisingly, he makes no direct mention of it in his pamphlet, but there is perhaps a coded reference. He tells the story of how the Reverend Tomkins was hounded out of the village, and goes on to say that he had been treated even worse and by 'the same class of people'. He added:

> If they burnt me and my little dog, that would be sure to give satisfaction! Dreadful crime in these villages to keep a little dog, but I think it's hard to hang a man for it. [9]

It seems as though, in this sentence, he has woven together death by burning, symbolised by the effigy-burning, and the possibility that in real life he might have hung if he had been found guilty of killing John Perryman.

And the others? Eliza, pregnant and alone with her three children? Amos three doors down, with his humiliated wife and family? What a situation. How do you cope? How, next day and the day after, do you face the village? All we know for sure is that the following January, Amos French, who had been so calm throughout the legal proceedings, was charged at Honiton by P. C. Martin with being drunk in Branscombe on 2 December 1884. He admitted the charge, then said in his defence that he had 'been a teetotaler for the best part of ten years, but was driven to take the drink by the conduct of some neighbours'. [10]

In Flora Thomson's account, the adulterers at Juniper Hill quickly left the village. Amazingly, and courageously, both Eliza with her little family, and Amos with his, stayed, and somehow put their lives back together.

Others who had been dragged into the inquest or criminal proceedings over John Perryman's death, though not burnt in effigy or dogged by suspicion, nevertheless soon left Branscombe. David Pile must have fiercely resented the way his private life was put on display in court. He had done his best to protect the accused and may have suffered for it. Other troubles soon came upon him. In March 1884 he had to undergo another inquest, held at the Masons Arms. This time the body was that of his sixteen-month-old son and the verdict was 'accidental death', for the little boy had died some six weeks after being scalded in an accident in January. [11] Later in 1884 he received 8s in outdoor relief because of sickness in the family.[12] In the general election of 1885 he was one of the few villagers to declare that he would vote Liberal, perhaps from disaffection as much as conviction. In 1886 he was on outdoor relief again because of family sickness. No doubt his family troubles were compounded by the difficulty of getting work, and he soon left. By 1891, aged 50, he was working as a coal miner at Gelligaer, near Merthyr Tydfil in South Wales, living there with his wife and two children.

Isaac French too, the 'blabbermouth' who had been publicly shamed by the Coroner, left the village in August 1886. An auction of his effects[13] included 'a very useful cross-bred mare', 7 years old, and a 'van with cover, in excellent condition' (plate 10). Isaac French and his wife also headed for South Wales, where he already had a married son living at Newport, and in 1891 he was a market gardener in Cardiff.

Was this the end of it? After Dowell left, did the village slowly calm down? No — one more piece of the puzzle has still to be put in place.

PART SEVEN

CONCLUSIONS

CHAPTER SEVENTEEN

Who Killed John Perryman?

Murder or accident?

It would be presumptuous at this distance of time to think we could solve the mystery of John Perryman's death. But across that distance some scraps of information have filtered down to us that do not appear in the published accounts. So it is worth reconsidering the possible explanations for this sad and baffling event.

Two explanations were current both before and after the inquiries had run their course. Either it was wilful murder, the intended victim being either John Perryman or, much more probably, someone for whom he was mistaken, or else it was a shooting accident. Let us begin with the theory of mistaken identity.

The notion that David Pile was the intended victim was thoroughly destroyed in court and at the inquest, if only because Pile's homeward path seldom took him over Culverwell Hill, and that he went by whatever route offered him a chance of company. No credible motive for Dowell to kill Pile was ever shown, and the tone of aggrieved and injured innocence in Dowell's pamphlet could not, in our view, have been feigned. Amos French might have had a motive to kill Pile and his alibi was not strong, but the same objections to a narrowly timed ambush at a predictable spot rule him out.

There was only one other person whose use of the Old Pits path was regular enough to make him a possible intended victim, namely William Bartlett, a man who has not appeared since Chapter One. But the fact that he normally accompanied John Perryman argues against this, for (as in Pile's case) who would lay an ambush for somebody who is likely to have a witness with him? We know of nothing that suggests a reason to kill Bartlett, and though one cannot be positive, he seems an unlikely target. If we rule him out, we are left with the choice between deliberate killing of Perryman and an accident.

If this were a detective novel, the argument relied on at the time, that no one could possibly have had a reason to kill so good and popular a man as Perryman, could easily be undermined. Likewise, in a murder mystery Bartlett's staying behind to collect firewood would look suspicious, and suggest either collusion with, or persuasion by, someone who wanted Perryman to be alone. And it is not difficult to think of other ingenious 'solutions'. But this happened in real life, and it seems far-fetched to attribute dark secrets or dangerous knowledge to Perryman, or to imagine a conspiracy that involved Bartlett.

Was there any evidence to suggest murder, rather than accident? First, there was the 'impression' made in the brambles and furze by somebody lying in wait (somewhat uncomfortably, it must be said), and secondly, the improbability that a gun fired by accident at 25 yards or more would have hit Perryman, and hit him in the upper body. But the 'impression' could have been made by someone lying in wait for a rabbit. As for the second point, if the victim appeared over a bank at which the gun was pointing when it accidentally went off, this fatal result appears less freakish.

If not murder, then an accident. And if by accident, was it done inadvertently by someone legitimately out shooting — i.e. someone with a gun licence and shooting rights — or by someone with no right to be there, that is, a poacher?

When P. C. Martin and Dowell conferred together at the site of the shooting, their first thought was that it might be one of the sons of farmer Amos Power. He was the tenant of Culverwell Farm, which included Old Pits, and his sons may have held gun licences. But they were quickly ruled out, and so was Skinner, the game-keeper at Beckham. According to Martin, Dowell also mentioned 'Mr Gill' as a gun-owner. The title 'Mr' suggests he might have meant George Gill, a dairyman who had rented Culverwell Farm from Amos Power. But by 1883 his lease had come to an end, and they seemed unable to think of any other legitimate hunters.

Dowell was convinced that it was a poaching accident, as were those closest to John Perryman. Yet, as we have seen, this was not the majority view, either before or after the inquiry. The Coroner's opinion was that once a man had been charged with murder, a poacher who had killed by accident would have come forward and confessed, and since no one had, it was probably murder. The jury was persuaded by this, but we doubt that conscience is always that powerful. People in the village today on whom we have tried out this argument agree with us — although we have to recognize that the influence of church and chapel, and the fear of divine retribution, would have been stronger then than now.

It was also said that nobody would go poaching on a 'common' across which labourers were known to come home in the dark. But, as Dowell wrote, John Perryman's brother James

> said he heard a gun fired in the same place where his brother was shot on the Wednesday previous, and about the same time at night. It was also heard the same night that the deceased was shot by an adjoining farmer about a quarter of an hour before the fatal shot, for it was nothing rare to hear guns on this hill. [1]

Neither Loveridge nor Tidwell was unduly surprised to hear the shot that killed Perryman. Only Bartlett said he had never heard any shots there.

Richard Lethaby also dismissed the poaching accident theory, with the objection that

> Poachers who go out with guns at night are men accustomed to their use, and are not likely to mistake a man for a bird, rabbit or hare, at a short distance. [2]

The reader can test the force of this argument against the plausibility of the story we tell later in this chapter.

Burn the Snob

If someone was poaching on Culverwell Hill that night, who might it have been? The police were right about one thing, that the fastest escape route was down through Collick's field to the cottages below.

This makes John Northcott, who lived at the western end of Upper Church, a possible suspect. In 1871, before P. C. Martin's time, he was charged and fined at Honiton for poaching a rabbit. [3] Unfortunately the newspaper report does not mention his method, so we cannot conclude that he owned a gun. But it is noticeable that during Bill Dowell's and Eliza Williams's visits to the Northcotts' house in the hour before the shooting, only Mrs Northcott seemed to be at home. John was at home for the 1881 census, and listed as resident on the 1885 electoral roll, so the question of his whereabouts on 8 September 1883 is not an idle one. However, nothing in the contemporary accounts points to him as the culprit.

There is one clue to a possible culprit. It does not appear in the documentary record, and has only come to light because Bill Carpenter remembered the words of Agnes Ward (see Appendix D). According to her, Bill Dowell, Eliza Williams and Amos French were not the only ones burned in effigy. There was a fourth person. She did not name him, she simply said that 'a close neighbour of Mrs Williams, who was in the habit of giving the children sweets, was given the same treatment'. This fourth person, she added, 'was greatly distressed to hear the shout "Burn the snob" from the cliff top. "It went through me like a knife," he said', and the result was tragedy. For 'this preyed on his mind so that eventually he hanged 'isself from a tree'. Bill Carpenter is sure that the tree was just behind Windycott, in the drangway at the entrance to Collick's field.

The clue is in 'burn the snob', because 'snob' is a dialect word for a cobbler or shoemaker. Who was a close neighbour to Eliza Williams, and a cobbler? Only Sam Parrett. He lived in the eastern end of Collick's Cottage (now Windycott), three doors up from Eliza, just across the drangway to Collick's field. The trustworthiness of Agnes Ward's recollection was quickly established, for the burial register shows that Samuel Parrett was buried 'by Coroner's order' on 20th January 1885. So there had been an inquest, something was amiss. And the death certificate, when obtained from the General Register Office, confirmed that he 'hanged himself' on the 14th January.

<table>
<tr><td>Fourteenth January 1885 Branscombe R. S. D.</td><td>Samuel Parrett</td><td>Male</td><td>58 Years</td><td>Shoemaker</td><td>Hanged himself whilst temporarily insane</td><td>Certificate received from Chas. E. Cox Deputy Coroner for Devon. Inquest held 17th January 1885</td><td>Twenty third January 1885</td></tr>
</table>

The importance of this corroboration can hardly be overstated. For it means we can be confident that the burning of the four effigies, of which there is no other record, actually happened. And the date of Parrett's suicide early in January 1885, after a spell of anguish, also points towards the previous November as a likely time for the effigy-burning. Just as with Dowell's testimony that the Reverend Tomkins was burned in effigy, it may seem surprising that such spectacular and memorable events as these burnings have been air-brushed from the village's collective and official memories. Perhaps a later generation felt they were too primitive and harmful to the village's reputation. Perhaps people felt ashamed of them.

Why does Sam Parrett suddenly appear in the story, and why was he burnt in effigy a year after the hearing? The reason given to Agnes as a little girl — that he had given sweets to Eliza's children — was the sort of reason one gives to an inquisitive child. But it does suggest how isolated Eliza must have been, if giving sweets to her children could be passed off, even to a child, as an offence that merited being burnt in effigy.

But if effigies of the three accused were burnt by people who still thought them guilty of Perryman's murder, why did Sam Parrett burn alongside them? No suggestion of complicity was made at the magistrates' court or the inquest on Perryman. His brother Henry

THE PARRETT FAMILY

The Parrett family, carpenters and shoemakers, settled in Branscombe in the eighteenth century. Three brothers Henry (1783-1853), a carpenter, John (1792-1875), a shoemaker, and Joseph (1796-1867) all lived near the church.

On the 1840 tithe map Henry, the eldest, appears as copyholder of three cottages in what is now the northern part of the churchyard. John, the second brother, served as sexton and lived at Church House. He also had a copyhold on two cottages further down the road, and two plots in what is now the southern part of the churchyard. He was followed as sexton by his son and grandson, John (1818-1883) and John (1848-1917), both shoemakers, the last of them also organist.

The third brother Joseph, a shoemaker, lived at Collick's Cottage, but owned no property. His two sons, Samuel (1826-1883) and Henry Saunders (1830-1899), were shoemakers. Samuel — the Sam Parrett who was burned in effigy — married Julianna Seaward Butter (1826-1893) in 1853, when both were 27, and they lived at Lower Church. She was the daughter of Oliver Butter (1795-1876), the baker at Bridge. They had no children. The couple moved into Collick's Cottage after his father's death in 1867. Although Sam had one apprentice in 1871, he had none in 1881, and Julianna was assisting her husband as 'boot binder'.

His younger brother, Henry Saunders Parrett, who gave evidence on the last day of the inquest, lived at Lower Church, and became a Methodist. He too was a shoemaker, assisted by his wife as boot-binder. He had no apprentice, but unlike Sam he rented a cliff plat.

Saunders Parrett had left no doubt that whatever gun had been used to shoot Perryman, it was not his, so the association could not have come about that way. Perhaps there were people in the village who, for some reason that we cannot discover, now thought that he was implicated in the murder. Or else, as the explanation given to Agnes Ward suggests, he might have been thought guilty by association for befriending his ostracized neighbours at Upper Church. Or possibly, following a quite different line of reasoning, those who believed in the innocence of Dowell had come to think that Sam Parrett was the man who accidentally shot Perryman, and they wanted to shame him into confessing. Whatever the motive, Sam Parrett's suicidal reaction suggests that he might indeed have been hiding a guilty secret, and feared he had been found out.

We have argued that the effigy-burning might not have had a single cause. Some people would have felt that Bill, Eliza and Amos had not been exonerated by the magistrates, others would have been shocked by sexual misconduct, and where Bill was concerned there might have been a political motive. To these we now add a fourth, very separate motive, that those who believed the shooting of Perryman was accidental wanted to force a confession.

Was any evidence brought to the inquest which might have drawn attention to Parrett? There were in fact two items, but not much notice was taken of either. One was the leather gun-wad found at the scene of the shooting, which could have suggested that the gun which killed Perryman had been fired by a leather-worker. Its significance had been overlooked at the inquest once Henry Parrett's gun, whose stock was 'bound around with a "wax-end" used by shoemakers', was dismissed as irrelevant. Some of the jury went as far as to doubt that the wad fitted Henry Parrett's gun-barrel, but it does not seem to have occurred to anyone to consider the wad separately from the gun. If it had, the possibility that another shoemaker was involved might have become apparent.

The other pointer was in Sarah Northcott's evidence, taken towards the end of a long sitting, when attention may have been wandering. The Northcotts' house was next to the Parretts', separated from it by the drangway into Collick's field, and the questioning went like this:

De Schmid: Did you see anyone pass up the road between eight and nine o'clock?

Mrs Northcott: Yes.

De Schmid: Can you tell us who it was?

Mrs Northcott: No; I saw a figure, but I don't know who it was. It might have been a quarter to nine o'clock. I saw the figure pass from Mr Samuel Parrett's linhay door. It went up the hill.

Under further questioning she said:

I did not think anything of it, because I had seen Mrs. Parrett there shutting her door on many occasions. I could not see whether it was a man or a woman. It was not a child. I did not know where the figure went, except that it went up the hill …

De Schmid: How far were you away from this shadow or figure?

Mrs Northcott: I don't know. I can't say who it was, or I should say … The figure was only about 10 or 12 paces away. I was certain it did not cross the road and go into the meadow below.

Mr Every: Did you not think it extraordinary to see a figure where you did?

Mrs Northcott: I have seen people standing about there before. *(In answer to the Coroner)* It might have been 20 minutes or half-an-hour before she heard the report that Perriman had been shot that she saw the figure.

The account is unclear. Parrett's linhay was on the side of his house and faced Mrs Northcott's house, so it would have been very easy for her to see 'a figure pass from Mr. Samuel Parrett's linhay door'. When she said the figure went 'up the hill' she may have meant either that the person went up the road, or that it went up the drangway between the two houses into Collick's field – i.e. up towards the trespassers' path and the site of the killing. Hence no doubt Every's pointed question, but the Coroner intervened and the ambiguity was never resolved. The interest of de Schmid and others present was fixed on the possibility that this figure might have been Dowell, sneaking out to kill Pile. Mrs Northcott, like most of the village witnesses, sounds very reluctant to get anyone into trouble. It seems almost unbelievable that at ten or twelve paces, in bright moonlight, she could not even tell whether the figure was a man or a woman, or whether it was or was not her neighbour.

A suggestion, not a solution

Rewriting history means trying to tell a more believable story than those already told. This is partly a matter of asking new questions, reassessing old evidence and searching for new, and recognising and avoiding bias. But it may also be a matter of imagining things differently. The story we present now is an imaginary construction of what might have happened on the night of the 8th September 1883. It is the nearest we can come to a solution to the Perryman mystery, but it is only a suggestion. We cannot prove it.

Sam Parrett, who was middle-aged and poor, may have been in the habit of slipping out through his linhay door with a gun — his brother, also a cobbler, owned a gun, so why not he? — and then making his way up round Collick's field and along the 'trespassers' path' through Culverwell Hill Coppice towards Old Pits, hoping to shoot a rabbit for Sunday dinner. On this fine Saturday night he sets out fairly late, knowing that Perryman and Bartlett come home that way, but he underestimates how long they would be kept at work, getting in the last of the harvest before the Sabbath.

Beyond the coppice he comes out on a grassy slope with scrubby bushes, where rabbit scuts bob away in the moonlight. He stops some twenty-five yards short of the low bank marking the boundary of the pits, where he knows there's a rabbit warren, loads his gun, and rams in one of the leather wads he's made at his workbench. Then, throwing his coat over a low-growing patch of furze and brambles, he lies down on it and waits for a rabbit to reappear. He is looking uphill, with his gun cocked and his finger on the trigger.

Suddenly he hears something, or somebody — he can't be sure — and then a large, pale, almost ghostlike apparition rears up in the moonlight over the bank ahead. He's badly startled, and makes an involuntary movement which jerks the gun upward so that the trigger presses against his finger. The moment it goes off, he realises that he has shot someone. Then, to his horror, as the man staggers down the bank towards him, even before he falls a few feet away in a patch of moonlight, he realises that he has shot John Perryman. John Perryman — the man that everyone, himself included, likes and admires! Has Perryman seen him? Has he been recognized? Sam Parrett is no hero, and his panicked reaction is to flee. He jumps up, grabs his coat, and hurries back home.

When he has got his breath back and stopped shaking, he tells his wife Julianna that he's been busy outside, perhaps tidying in the garden or the linhay. As the hue and cry intensifies he has to pretend shock and sorrow. He can't avoid John Perryman's funeral four days later, held in the church because those wishing to attend were too numerous for the chapel, and in response to appeals from the pulpit from a visiting Methodist minister and the Reverend Swansborough, he almost blurts out the truth. But after that, with every passing day it seems more and more impossible to confess. The protracted hearings in the school torture him with anxiety. The leather gun-wad! Discussing the case with his brother is terrible, and he avoids it as much as possible. Fortunately he and his wife are known as a reclusive couple, so he can keep his head down without exciting comment.

He is relieved at the verdict of 'wilful murder', for he's not quarrelsome and would never be a suspect. He's even more relieved that his neighbours are exonerated, though it also suits him that many in the village still think them guilty. But his conscience torments him with what he's done, and with what he's put them through, and he's ashamed of his cowardice. He can't face going to church on Sundays, and finds excuses. Perhaps he even tries to make up a little for what he's done by being nice to Eliza when many are not, and giving sweets to her children. But he knows that Dowell and his supporters are on the hunt for someone who might have been poaching on Old Pits and accidentally shot Perryman, and he fears it's only a matter of time before he is accused.

A whole year goes by like this. It's a relief when Bill Dowell leaves, but then comes Bonfire Night. A noisy procession making rough music comes marching down the road and stops somewhere outside. His curtains are drawn, he won't allow Julianna to look. After an age, it seems, they march off, down through the churchyard and up the hill to the cliff-top. A bonfire blazes behind the trees on the skyline, and suddenly shouts come across the valley: 'Burn the snob! Burn the snob!' His guilt pierces him like a knife through the heart, and he breaks down. Eventually he confesses to Julianna, who is distraught but loyal. The weeks pass by, he stays indoors, he's sure people look at him contemptuously, and in the end he feels nothing but contempt for himself. One night he takes a rope from the linhay, throws it over a branch of the small tree in the lane, knots it, climbs up the bank and swings off.

The widow

Now we return to facts we can establish. Julianna was prostrated by Sam's suicide, and from 1885 onwards she was receiving outdoor relief of 2s 6d a week on grounds of 'total disability'. Sometime after the inquest and burial, she moved to Grapevine where she lived alone in one of the smaller cottages. [4] Ephraim Perryman and his family were neighbours, which cannot have been comfortable. She was still there in 1891 but shortly thereafter was taken to Honiton workhouse, apparently with a broken thigh.

While bedridden there she became, according to Henry Key, master of the workhouse, violent and noisy, and suffered from delusions, 'constantly trying to crawl from her bed ... to make an attack on someone'. Dr T. W. Shortridge certified that she 'endeavours to get away from imaginary people who are going to do her an injury' — fantasies that must have expressed the way she had felt for the last eight years. She was transferred to Exminster Asylum in August 1893, suicidal and suffering from dementia and epilepsy. She died after a few days at Exminster, a late victim of the shooting at Old Pits. [5]

The headstone

We do not know who were the moving spirits behind the Methodist campaign to erect a headstone for John Perryman, though they must have included his brother James and his son Robert. They were less vindictive than the jury at the inquest, and made a point of setting in stone their own view of how he died:

In
Loving Memory
Of
JOHN PERRYMAN
AGED 67 YEARS
FOR MANY YEARS SUPERINTENDENT
OF THE WESLEYAN METHODIST
SCHOOL
IN THIS PARISH

WHO WAS ACCIDENTLY SHOT DEAD ON
CULVERHOLE HILL ON THE EVENING OF
SATURDAY SEPTR 8th 1883
WHILST RETURNING FROM WORK IN THE HARVEST FIELD

The memory of the just is blessed

Sudden death Sudden glory

This stone was erected by some who
knew Him as a tribute of affection and love

JOHN PERRYMAN
AGED 67 YEARS
IN THIS PARISH
HILL ON THE EVENING OF
1885

CHAPTER EIGHTEEN

Epilogue

Despite Sam Parrett's suicide, and the new gravestone in the churchyard declaring that John Perryman had been shot by accident, the belief that his death was a murder gone wrong, and that Dowell was somehow implicated, remained strong. [1] Older people, telling the story in recent years, still reproduced versions of it. Lily Gush (1901-1992), who remembered her parents telling her about the 'murder', still seemed to think that Dowell was the murderer:

> They said he was a nice young man. Got around. ... Some older people heard the man say 'I shot the wrong man!' He was going to shoot the man who got his sister in trouble ... He thought he wasn't no good, and he wasn't ... Oh dear, dear... [2]

Phoebe Spencer, who had read Dowell's pamphlet, said 'He was not exactly violent, but he was a very prejudiced man. You can tell by his article [pamphlet.]' [3] So, given these doubts, what was life like in later years for the three who had been accused and acquitted?

Bill Dowell

Bill Dowell wrote most of his pamphlet in 1884 'here in my lodgings, 6 Hindsley-place, Forest Hill, London'. [4] It was published early in 1885 and, according to Bill Carpenter, 'was regarded as scandalous by the local people to whom it paid no compliments'. [5] Dowell sent a copy to Richard Lethaby, who gave an impressive endorsement to what he called

> a plain and straightforward narrative, just issued by Dowell, the accused murderer. That the young man is bitterly indignant at the treatment he received, is not surprising,

having spent his hard-earned savings in defence, and been treated as a suspected felon; but his little book bears the imprint of truthfulness, and should have the effect of rousing public attention to the injustice he has suffered. ... It is a sad, sad tale, from beginning to end, but one we would heartily commend to our readers, not doubting that the result of their perusal will be their moral certainty that whoever shot John Perryman, whether by accident or design, it was not William Dean Dowell. [6]

Lethaby, who had previously dismissed the idea of accidental death, now acknowledged the possibility. He added that the pamphlet could be bought for threepence from Dowell at 6 Hindsley Place, but he probably received few orders.

Bill Dowell had said he was going to start a new life in Australia, but if he went he cannot have stayed there long. The 1891 census found him in his old haunts in Forest Hill, working again as a carpenter and joiner and living in lodgings at 23 Davids Road (now demolished).

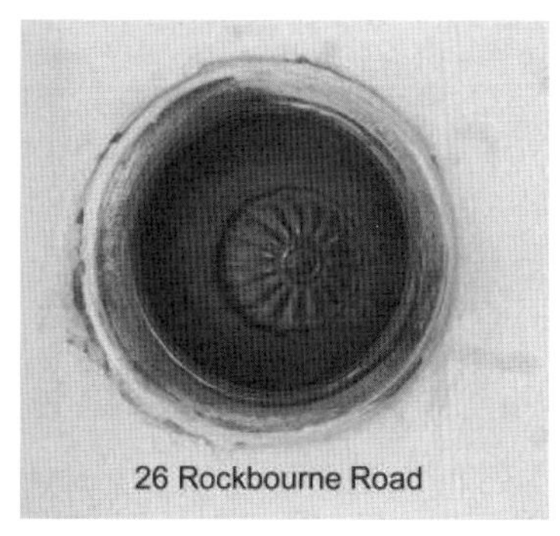
26 Rockbourne Road

There was, it seems, no hope of a reconciliation with Susan Ann, for on 12 June 1892 he married Wilhelmine Gercke, a German immigrant. He was 39, she 27. The censuses of 1901 and 1911 show them living in Forest Hill, at the nostalgically named Branscombe Villa, otherwise 26 Rockbourne Road. The house still exists, a comfortable semi-detached villa, probably built some twenty or thirty years earlier as part of the rapid expansion of the suburb of Lewisham. Dowell continued in his old trade and there would have been plenty of work, for houses and public buildings were springing up all around him.

His brothers Fred and Lewis lived close by, each with a household of children, and their fish and poultry shop flourished at 36-38 Perry Vale. [7] Bill and Wilhelmine had three daughters — Amelia, Eunice and Grace — and one son, William Dean. One can imagine that their life in Edwardian London was comfortable enough, with family gatherings and outings in the nearby parks and countryside. But as with so many other families, the First World War intervened and everything changed. William Dean junior, a private in the Machine Gun Corps, was killed in May 1917 on the Western Front. He was 22 years old. Bill lived on to be 78, and died in 1930. Wilhelmine, who died in 1942, would have seen planes from her native country drop bombs on London in yet another war.

Wilhelmine presumably knew that Bill was paying maintenance for his daughter Flossie in Branscombe, but did Bill and his new family ever invite her to London or go back to the village to see her? It seems unlikely, though we know that at least one of his brothers returned to the village from time to time. [8] But we do know that Bill worried about Flossie, and that his mother sent him news of her. We have been given a copy of a touching letter that he wrote to Flossie for her twelfth birthday: [9]

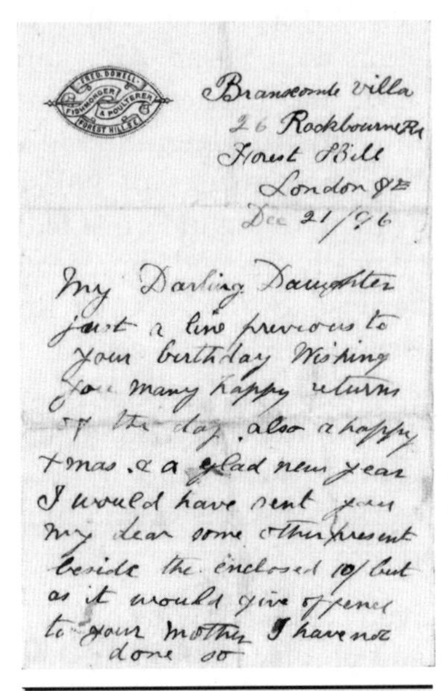

Branscombe villa
26 Rockbourne Rd
Forest Hill
London S/E
Dec 21/96

My Darling Daughter
just a line previous to
your birthday wishing
you many happy returns
of the day, also a happy
Xmas, & a glad new year
I would have sent you
my dear some other present
beside the enclosed 10/- but
as it would give offence
to your Mother I have not
done so
I would like my dear to
get a line from you
with or without your
Mothers consent, as I often
am afraid your life
is not a happy one
altough my Mother told
you was allright but
would like it confirmed
by yourself we are having
some very bad weather here
I now conclude with
best love to you from
your old Father
Will Dean Dowell
XXXXX
XXXX
May God bless you my
Darling & prosper
You in this life & heaven XX
at last

A loving letter, and from the sound of it, not the first or last, although it seems communication was sporadic. Flossie's mother, Susan Ann Gill, was obviously hostile. No doubt she had also heard that he was married, and to a much younger woman.

By 1891 Susan Ann and Flossie had moved from The Fountain Head to Yew Tree cottage, on the other side of the road, so that she could keep house for her father, John Gill. Flossie grew up in this rather strange household, with her mother, three carpenter uncles and the old man, who lived to be 89 and died in 1911. But before his death Susan Ann had moved back to The Fountain Head to keep house once again for her brother Thomas. We catch a glimpse of her in a letter of 1907, thanking her for helping out at a social evening held in Branscombe by the Primrose League. [10] The League was a Conservative party offshoot; most innkeepers at that period were loyal Tories, and Susan Ann had evidently been doing her bit for the party.

If Flossie had been left to keep house for her uncles and grandfather at Yew Tree cottage, she soon escaped. For in June 1908, aged 24, she married William Ackland at Honiton. A shotgun wedding probably, for their first child Ruby was born on June 21st. William was the eldest son of the farmer at Higher Weston, also named William Ackland. [11] To begin with the couple lived at Weston, William working for his father, but after the birth of another daughter, Dorothy, in 1910, they moved to The Lamb inn in Honiton. William became the landlord, Flossie assisted, and Ruby, aged two, stayed behind in Branscombe, living with her grandmother Susan Ann at The Fountain Head. A son Leslie was born in Honiton in 1914. Then came the war, and William went off to fight. He returned safely, only to die in the flu epidemic of 1918. Susan Anne died the same year, perhaps from the same cause.

Flossie, motherless and widowed with three young children, continued to manage the Lamb until her son Leslie took over from her, and when she retired she lived with her married daughter Ruby Chapman in Hampshire. We do not know if she ever met her father in later life.

Amos French

Amos French seems to have lived down the suspicion and scandal that provoked his uncharacteristic binge in December 1884. He stayed on as Henry Ford's tenant at Upper Church, continuing to live just down the road from Eliza. His wife Elizabeth, David Pile's sister, died in 1905 aged 74. Amos died seven years later, in 1912, aged 80.

Eliza Williams

Eliza also stayed on in the village. Her husband Thomas remained in Exminster Asylum, and his body was brought back to be buried in Branscombe in 1895. He was only 46. Eliza never remarried, but she seems to have become happily reintegrated into village life, largely by becoming a member of the Methodist congregation. She had started life as a church-goer, but changed her allegiance after the traumas of 1883-4, finding chapel people more supportive than the Reverend Swansborough's flock. She may also have been influenced by the Devon and Dorset Methodist Mission, set up in 1888, and by the arrival in Branscombe, shortly afterwards, of two female evangelists. Eliza's son Peter and Amos French's grandson Roland, two 'young lads' in their teens, were among their converts [12] and it seems likely that Eliza and her daughters Lily (Lilian) and little Ellen joined the chapel at about the same time. Eliza appears in Methodist group photographs taken at the turn of the century (Plate 12).

In the census of 1891 Peter and his elder brother Algernon, aged 13 and 15, were still at home, working as farm labourers, but they soon took off, part of a generational shift away from the land. They worked as insurance agents and Algernon made insurance his career. Peter went on to train at a theological college, became a Methodist minister, moved to South Africa, and was President of the Methodist Movement in Cape Town. He had a large family and died out there.

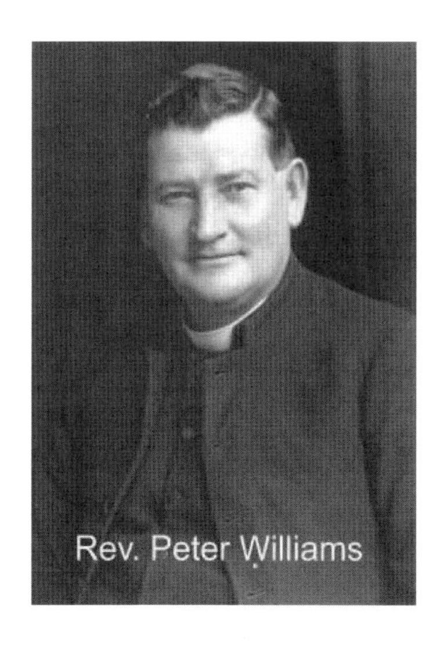

Rev. Peter Williams

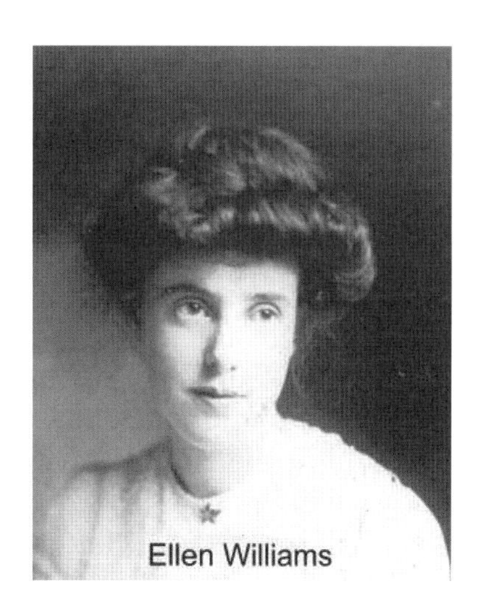

Ellen Williams

When she was seventeen, Eliza's younger daughter Ellen was sent to join Algernon in Torquay. From there she moved to Manchester, where she was manageress of a photographic shop. Eventually, she returned to Torquay, became engaged to a young Methodist, Charles Cload, and they were married at Branscombe, in the grand new chapel.

By 1902 Peter had bought the four Upper Church cottages for £255 from his cousin Fred Williams, to provide a home for his mother Eliza and her sister Laura. They moved into the more commodious house now known as Country House, but then called Plantation View because a new wood had been planted on the hillside opposite. Laura, who never married and who later became blind, bought the two easternmost cottages in 1924, and let them to the three unmarried Parrett sisters who ran a tea-shop, selling 'cream teas smelling of paraffin'.

While Eliza went up the road to chapel on Sundays, Laura, being a teacher at the Church school, walked down to St Winifred's. The sisters carried their denominational difference over into politics: Eliza became a keen Liberal and Laura a staunch Conservative. At election times there would be separate Liberal and Conservative meeting rooms in Plantation View, one each side of the front door. The household had a reputation for cheerfulness: there used to be a melodeon [13] for dancing in the upper room known, perhaps for historic reasons, as the cider bar. The room had an old smuggler's door out into Collick's field. According to Bill Carpenter, Eliza acquired the nickname 'Bulldog', and was inordinately fond of chudleighs and cream.

When Eliza died in 1937, her daughter Lily moved in to look after Laura. After Laura's death in 1943 the two western cottages were sold for £500, while the other two passed on in the family until they were sold in the 1970s. Thus ended the connection of the Williams family with Upper Church, which had lasted for nearly a century and a half, ever since Matthew Williams laundered his smuggling profits there in 1830. By now the two families, Dowells and Williams, had spread far and wide, and the village had become a very different place.

At rest

We found Bill Dowell's address in Rockbourne Road in the census of 1911, and we knew that he died in 1930. Had he moved house in the meantime? And where was he buried?

The principal municipal cemetery for Lewisham is at Hither Green. When we arrived at the office, the secretary, well used to people searching for ancestral graves, consulted her digitised lists - and found William Dean Dowell at Ladywell, a cemetery opened in 1858 and now disused. We saw from the entry in her large ledger that he lived in Rockbourne Road until his death.

OF LEWISHAM. 64

[CEMETERY.

and 17 Vic., Cap. 134, and the other Acts incorporated therein.

What Monumental Distinction?	Date and Particulars of Sum paid for Erection of Monuments, &c., and for keeping same in Repair, &c.	£	s.	d.	Name and Description of the Deceased.	When buried.	No. of the Interment in Register of Burials.
Recumbent cross and curb on landing by Chappell	1931 Aug 10				Wm D. Dowell Husband of Wilhelmine Dowell	1930 Sept 6	69890

His wife Wilhelmine bought the grave, adorned with a recumbent stone cross, and both he and she, along with their eldest daughter Amelia and her husband, were buried there. Grave no. 3653 in plot D. We were shown a plan of the numbered graves: 'It's a second-class burial, so it's not in the first two rows by the path', said the secretary, 'and you may not find it. It's very overgrown.'

She was right, it *was* overgrown. The council, making the best of it, advertise Ladywell cemetery as a nature trail. We drove past a derelict Chapel of Ease, down less and less frequented paths to near where the Victorian cremation chimney poked up through trees. The section in which the Dowells were buried was on a low rise, half of which had gravestones showing amidst the tall grasses, while the other half was given over to unmarked 'public' graves. Trees, wild roses and thistles grew between the graves and out of them, and we were pleasantly surprised to find big, succulent blackberries already ripe in July. As we picked and ate some, we suddenly noticed, beneath the brambles, a recumbent cross inscribed 'AT REST'. Clearing the grass from the kerbstones round the grave, we made out 'IN LOVING MEMORY OF' on one, but the kerbstone where the name should have been had fallen outwards and could not be read. A cornerstone,

however, bore the number 3653, so it definitely was the grave we were looking for.

We returned next day with a spade. At the first attempt to lever up the kerbstone, one of us glimpsed 'William', the other 'Dowell', before it fell back. At the second attempt, we read, in elegant lettering:

WILLIAM DEAN DOWELL

WHO DEPARTED THIS LIFE 1ST SEPTEMBER 1930 IN HIS 79TH YEAR

In the garden of happy memory there is always sunshine

The others — Wilhelmine, their daughter and their son-in-law — were not commemorated. Perhaps there was not enough money. We stood for a while, thinking about that strangely interrupted life, then went on our way.

APPENDIX A

Farming in Branscombe in the 1880s

Farms in Branscombe in the 1881 census

Farms are in descending order of acreage. Name of farm is followed by name of farmer; farmer's age; household composition; farm acreage; number of workers; farmer's place of birth; and those owned by Henry Ford (HF). [1]

1. Edge Barton: John Pile 47 (wife, two children, sister-in-law, servant) 435 acres, 12 men/5 boys (Otterton)
2. Berry: William Pile 43 (wife, 5 children, servant) 289 acres, 3 men/1 boy (East Budleigh) HF
3. Higher Weston: James Richards 32 (wife, 4 children, servant) 250 acres, 4 labourers (Branscombe)
4. Coxe's: Joseph Tedbury 34 (wife, 7 children) 237 acres, 4 men (Otterton)
5. Lower Weston: John Ellis 34 (wife, 4 children, nephew) 236 acres, 7 men & boys (Broadhembury)
6. Elverway: Robert Power 83 (wife, 1 child, sister) 200 acres, 5 men (Southleigh)
7. Big Seaside 1: William Pike 74 (wife, I child, I servant) 200 acres, 5 men/2 boys (Upottery) HF
8. Higher Watercombe: Henry Hurley 66 (wife, 2 servants) 190 acres, 4 men/1 boy (Kilmington) HF
9. Rockenhayne: Amos Power 44 (wife, 3 children) 160 acres, 2 men/2 boys (Branscombe)
10. Gays: Robert Bartlett 68 (wife, 2 lodgers, servant) 138 acres, 6 men/2 boys (Beer) HF
11. Higher House: Luke Richards 31 (wife, 4 children, servant) 110 acres, 3 men/1 boy (Branscombe) HF
12. Mill: Emmanuel Pile 45 (wife, 5 children, servant) 106 acres, 2 men/1 boy (Southleigh) HF

13. Pitt: William Burrough 45 (sister, lodger) 100 acres, 2 men/2 boys (Otterton) HF
14. Woodhouse: Susan Dawe 64 (3 children) 90 acres, 1 man/2 boys (Otterton) HF
15. Hole: Henry Pike 28 (wife) 90 acres, 2 men/1 boy (Southleigh) HF
16. Weston: Thomas Groom 71 (wife, nephew, servant) 72 acres, 1 man (Whitchurch)
17. Church Living: James Somers 86 (2 children, 3 grandchildren) 70 acres, 1 man/1 boy (Branscombe) HF
18. Lower Bulstone: Robert Glyde 39 (wife, 5 children, servant) 68 acres, 1 man (Hawkchurch)
19. Higher Bulstone: John Harding 66 (wife) 35 acres, 1 labourer (Otterton) HF
20. Big Seaside 2: John Salter 61 (wife, 2 children, lodger) 13 acres (Ottery St Mary) HF

Note: *Henry Ford owned 12 of the 20 farms. Of the farmers, 16 were from neighbouring parishes (including 5 from Otterton). Most farm workers however were Branscombe-born.*

Farm labourers' income and expenditure

The Royal Commission on Labour in 1894 compiled a typical weekly budget for an agricultural worker's family with a man and his wife, one son working on a farm and several children aged 2 to 9.

Lamp oil	4d
Candles	5d
Tea, Sugar etc	2s 8d
Dairy produce	5s 6d
Flour	5d
Meat	4s 6d
Bread	5s 0d
Club money	11d
TOTAL	19s 9d

Rent is still to pay (2s 6d), so total outgoings, with nothing added for clothing, shoes or sickness, amount to £1 2s 3d.

Although the table was compiled in 1894, prices and wages had not changed much since the 1880s. The Royal Commission assumed an income of about £1. 5s a week, but in Devon wages were lower, supposedly made up by part-payment in cider. A farm-worker might earn 10s a week, his young son perhaps 7s. So we are actually talking about (assumed) outgoings of £1 2s 3d and income of 17s. [2] Small amounts might be added for lace-making, taking in visitors, bird-scaring, etc. Even so, the modest outlay tabled by the Royal Commission was beyond most families' means.

APPENDIX B

Foot-stepping the Shooting

Can we pinpoint the place where John Perryman was shot? The likely area can be narrowed down by following clues from each end: from Perryman's parting from Loveridge on Culverwell Hill, and from P. C. Martin's description of a murderer's route from Upper Church; also from where Tidwell and Williams heard cries for help and ran up from the village street.

We have described the paths that Perryman and Loveridge took from Edge Farm to the stile at the upper end of Pit Lane in Chapter 1 (see map, Figure 2). They are public footpaths and easy to follow. The problem starts where the two men parted company and Perryman turned left on to a small path going down through Old Pits (the enclosure marked 668 on the 1889 OS Map). The path that he took no longer exists, and the pits are overgrown and almost impassable. Lower down the hill, the enclosures above Blue Ball (664 and 667) are now woodland, 666 has become a fine, steeply sloping private garden, and the 'Three Acre' field (669), where the New Chapel was built in 1899-1900, has recently been re-landscaped. Only Collick's field above Upper Church terrace (673) is relatively unchanged, although it no longer contains allotments.

Robert Loveridge said that the last time he saw Perryman was 'about a quarter to nine o'clock, on the hill behind his house, walking in the direction of his home'. He said that he heard a gunshot about five minutes later but did not connect it with Perryman and continued on his way. [1] He heard no cries because by then Perryman was on the south-east side of the hill, out of earshot.

The 1889 Ordnance Survey map shows no paths through Old Pits. This is not surprising, as P. C. Martin mentioned that although there was a path going towards Edge Farm from Old Pits, it was not a public one. [2] On the other hand, the map shows a straight track or footpath at the lower (right) end of the pits (see Figure 5). It runs south-east through an area of scrub (667) and then through an enclosure called Culverwell Hill Coppice (670). Our first attempt to scramble from the stile at the upper end of Pit Lane down through Old Pits, using badger trails, brought us out at the top of this track. It ran straight on downhill, through what remains of the ancient hazel coppice, and brought us out on the sloping field (673) formerly known as Collick's, above Upper Church terrace.

Was this, we wondered, Perryman's way home? Would he have left the pits, headed through the coppice, walked down the side of Collick's field, and then dropped down into the steep gardens behind Grapevine?

This old postcard view shows Upper Church terrace (A), with Collick's cottage a little higher up (B). Then comes Grapevine (C), the new Chapel, built by 1900 (D), and Blue Ball (E), with Street in the distance. Culverwell Hill Coppice (F) and the scrubby grass hillside beyond are also visible, as are the allotments in Collick's field (G).

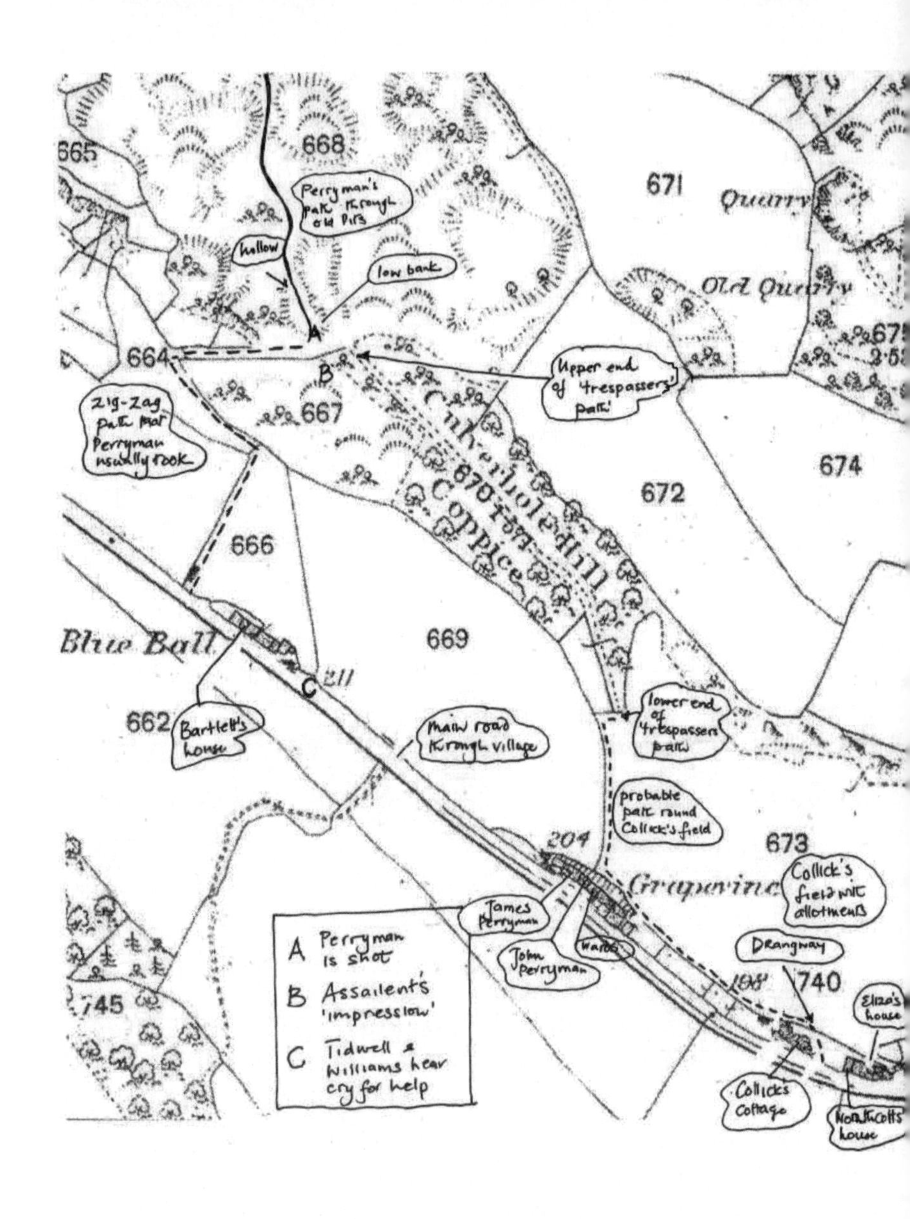

Figure 6: Pathways in the Old Pits and below

The fact that the evidence on the shooting mentions the pits, but not the coppice, indicates that Perryman was shot before he reached the coppice. But he must have been at the lower end of Old Pits, for he is said to have been 'within 100 yards of his cottage', which was 'only a gunshot below'. [3] On the other hand, another bit of evidence suggests that, even if he had not been shot, he would not have taken the coppice track. P. C. Martin speaks of 'a trespassers' path', by which he surely meant a different path from Perryman's normal path. Here is the description he gave to the Magistrates:

> I went to the spot where Perriman was killed … I saw the place where apparently someone had been lying down … I traced a track from the spot where the impression was on the ground through the furze to the Collick, which is the name for several potato plots belonging to many persons, among whom is French, but I could not distinguish the marks. The track was in the direction of the six cottages. I traced the tracks as far as behind the deceased's house.

A little later, cross-examined by Mr Every for the defence, he clarified:

> The path through the undergrowth from where the impression on the ground was he should call a trespassers'path. [4]

This 'trespassers' path' sounds very like our track through the coppice. He presumably called it a trespassers' path because the coppice, unlike the Old Pits, was not thought of as common land. Martin indicates that it was overgrown, so it was seldom used, and was unlikely to have been Perryman's normal way home.

Back to the OS map. On our first scrambling walk we had noticed a possible track running westwards and down-slope from the top of the 'trespassers' path'. Since it was going away from Grapevine and Upper Church we had ignored it. But looking at the old OS map there seemed to be the remnants of a fenced trackway, and Celia Andrews, who lives at No. 3 Blue Ball, down below, affirmed that there had been a track or path up through the woods above her garden, but after the great storm of 1988 trees had fallen across it, making it impassable.

Not quite impassable: we set off up through her steep garden (666), then followed for a short way a small track running west alongside an old earthen bank. We came to a wide opening on our right, from which an old track set off at an acute angle eastwards up the hill. It was much overgrown, but still had a border of stones. We turned up it and after a short while, as we had hoped, reached the top of the 'trespassers' path' with Old Pits on our left. Eileen Carpenter later confirmed that she could remember a 'right of way' up the hillside beside Blue Ball which led to Old Pits — apparently the very path that we had re-found — so the gated entrance to Celia Andrews' garden might once have allowed public access from the road. We shall refer to this as the 'zigzag path' (Figure 5).

Now things were beginning to fall into place! The old map suggests that there had been a fence close to the junction of the zigzag path with the trespassers' path. Down-slope to the south-east from here, in what is now woodland, would have been the scrubby grass hillside with the coppice beyond, while up-slope to the north-west was a low bank, and behind it, one of the old pits. John Perryman's path, as he approached the lower end of Old Pits, would have swung down into this pit, then up again on the further side (the pits are not particularly steep-sided). We imagine him breasting the slope as he climbs over the bank. Below him and slightly to his right, behind the fence, would have been the furze and bramble patch that P. C. Martin described. A man is lying there [5] with his gun trained on the bank. As Perryman looms up, a shot rings out. He staggers down the bank on to the flatter ground and collapses.[6]

This ties in with the report of Dr Evans' *post-mortem*, and with *Pulman's* summing up of this part of the story:

> Perryman was in the habit of taking a short cut to his house across Old Pits, which is a high hill covered with furze and brambles. The deceased parted with his companions before he reached Old Pits. When just within 50 yards of the brow of the hill, under which stands a row of thatched cottages, the

deceased had to walk over a high mound, down into a hollow, and up again on to the flat. It is conjectured that the person who fired the fatal shot was standing behind the fence, and that the gun was fired just as Perryman was rising from the hollow. [7]

What we imagine is that if the shot had not been fired, Perryman would have turned westwards down the zigzag path towards what was then a small meadow (664), then turned back eastwards and walked down to Blue Ball and then on down the road to his house at Grapevine.

His assailant, however, would have taken off in the opposite direction by the trespassers' path through Culverwell Hill Coppice, then skirted round the allotments in Collick's field to the gap between Collick's Cottage and Upper Church.

The *Exeter Flying Post* gave a succinct (though biased) account of the escape route:

> A path from this spot, but rarely used, bore evidence of having been traversed by the person who had lain in concealment, and the footsteps terminated at the back of the row of cottages in which the prisoners — and other persons — reside. [8]

P. C. Martin was more circumspect:

> He did not see any footmarks, but there was an indication of where a person had gone through the undergrowth. [9]

P. C. Martin and Superintendent de Schmid timed the walk from the 'impression' in the brambles to behind Grapevine, and from Grapevine to Northcott's cottage, which suggests that there was no diagonal path through the allotments in Collick's field, and that the assailant would have had to skirt round its lower edge.

Meanwhile, on the night of the shooting, William Henry Tidwell and William Williams were walking up the village road towards Street. They had walked about 200 yards beyond Grapevine and almost reached Blue Ball when they heard (as they might easily do, for noises are amplified in the narrow valley) a shout coming from further up the hill. They could not see anything, but if they raced up from Blue Ball by the zigzag path they would have found the dying man at the top. They must have carried him down to Grapevine by the same path, otherwise they would have obliterated the tracks which Martin saw the next day on the trespassers' path.

APPENDIX C

The 1885 Election in Branscombe

Background to the 1884 Reform Act and 1885 election.

- Disraeli's Conservative government fell in 1880, and Disraeli himself died in 1881. His Second Reform Act of 1867 had given the vote to male householders and £10 lodgers in towns.

- Gladstone, the new Liberal Prime Minister, was committed to extending the franchise to the countryside. In 1884 the Third Reform Act was passed, giving the vote to male householders and £10 lodgers in the counties. To get it past the Conservative majority in the House of Lords, Gladstone conceded a redistribution of seats.

- In July 1885 Joseph Chamberlain, Gladstone's President of the Board of Trade, published his Radical Programme which included manhood suffrage, progressive income tax, church disestablishment and land reform. As party divisions sharpened, Conservative Associations with local branches were set up in each constituency.

- The election in November 1885 was inconclusive. Gladstone's Liberals won the most seats, but without an overall majority. Irish Nationalists held the balance of power, and the Liberal Party split over Irish Home Rule.

- Another general election followed in 1886. Gladstone and the Home Rule Liberals lost to an alliance of Conservatives and Liberal Unionists, the latter led by Joseph Chamberlain.

Branscombe Methodists as Liberal voters.

People's voting intentions were marked in pencil on the Branscombe electoral roll for 1885, 'C' for Conservative, 'R' for Radical, and 'D' (probably) for 'declined to say'. Below are the names of those voters marked 'R' or 'D' who were listed as fathers in the Methodist baptism register (with place of abode in brackets):

1. George Butter (R), baker and Methodist preacher (Bridge).
2. Samuel Coombs (R), agricultural labourer (later shopkeeper) employed by Eliza Williams on her cliff plat (Street).
3. James Gush (R), agricultural labourer, 'a typical working-man local preacher'. Followed John Perryman as Superintendent of the Sunday school (Bank). [1]
4. William Harris (R), agricultural labourer, 'converted by the example of his first wife' (Cotte). [2]
5. Thomas Otton (R), tailor (Vicarage).
6. William Dowell (D), agricultural labourer, father of George Dowell, mentioned above (Vicarage).
7. James Gosling (D), cliff farmer and fisherman, married to Amos French's sister (Church).
8. Samuel Hutchings (D), gardener, father of the wife who converted William Harris (Barnells).
9. Robert Perryman (D) agricultural labourer, John Perryman's son (Street). [3]
10. John Taylor (D), agricultural labourer, whose son Charles was an active Methodist in the next generation (Street).

Conservative M.P.'s in East Devon.

The great majority of Branscombe men voted Conservative in the 1885 election, and in this the village was no different from the rest of East Devon. Before the Reform Act, local Tory landowners had regularly been elected — Sir John Kennaway since 1870, and Captain Walrond from 1880. After the 1885 election, when the constituency was divided, Kennaway continued as M.P. for Honiton (including Branscombe) until 1910, and Walrond was returned for Tiverton until 1906.

APPENDIX D

Oral History: Bill Carpenter's Account

The shooting of John Perryman occurred a hundred and twenty-five years ago, too long ago for there to be any first-hand accounts. But two people remember being told the story by Agnes Ward, who was a small girl at the time of the shooting. Terence Lee remembers that Agnes Ward said: 'Those of us in the village — we had a pretty good idea who did it, and the reason why'. But alas, she did not tell him who they thought it was.

Bill Carpenter remembers far more, and it is his account that we reproduce here. Bill was born in 1926 in Fulham, London. His father, Henry, was a policeman, his mother a Branscombe girl, Lily Alma Ward. As a baby, he was nearly 'gathered' with double pneumonia and was swiftly bundled down to stay with his aunt, Lucy Batten. His childhood was spent between London and Branscombe; during the war he went to the village school, and after the war he settled in the village. In 1961 he married Eileen Northcott. They live at Street.

Bill has a fantastic memory, and a passion for detail. He also has no truck with tape-recorders, so once he has told a story, he writes it down. His account of the Perryman affair is an amalgam of what he remembers from his conversation with Agnes Ward and his own research. His manuscript starts with a copy of the inscription on Perryman's tombstone. Then, on the same page, comes a rough plan of where the shooting occurred. After that there are three pages of writing. We also have another shorter, earlier account by him. Here we reproduce the longer account, written in 2002, but bring in a few details from the earlier one.

AGNES WARD

Agnes Ward was born in 1874 at Grapevine, the youngest of John and Jane Ward's six children. At the time of the shooting, her family lived next door to John Perryman. People remember her, and her stories.

> *Sheila Fisher*: Agnes Ward talked about how she and her mother and her sister made shirts for the men — great thick flannel shirts — for about a few pence, to make a living. Later on, her mother was on the parish. She was paid 2s a week by the Relieving Officer.

Much later, she ran the corner shop at Street that belonged to George Gill, and people remembered her there:

> *Joan Phillips:* She was a tall, wonderful old lady, very clean, tidy, always in a sort of darkie dress and in a pinafore apron, and she had lovely grey hair. She told us she never washed it, always brushed it.
>
> *Wynne Clarke:* She used to wear the old-fashioned little gold-rimmed glasses. She was a very strict old lady. [1]

Agnes Ward was a staunch Methodist and late in life wrote her own account of Methodism in Branscombe. She died in 1967, aged 93.

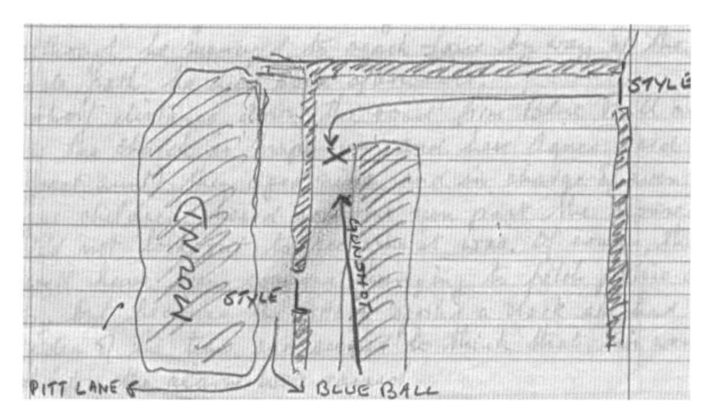

Bill Carpenter's sketch-map of the site of the shooting

FATAL SHOOTING ON THE OLD PITTS, BRANSCOMBE 1883

By Bill Carpenter

On the south side of Branscombe Church a stone raised to the memory of John Perryman, aged 67, tells us that he was accidentally shot dead on Culverhole Hill on the evening of Saturday September 8th 1883 whilst returning from work in the harvest field.

This statement is misleading. By all accounts the moon was full and it was as light as day, so that the shooting was almost certainly deliberate. It also tends to give the impression that it took place on the road near Windwhistle Gate, and that he died on the spot. This was not the way it happened.

Until the blight of the Common Market descended upon the land, [2] the terrain at the top of Pitt Lane was much the same as it was in 1883. It was a series of hillocks and uneven ground which was the result, and remains of old lime workings. Where there is now a gate on the western side was once a stile from which a path led beside a hedge to the end of a fern covered bank where it turned at a right angle and led between the bank and a hedge to another stile. From this stile one path led to Pitt Lane, and another down the hillside to the cottages at Blue Ball where John Perryman lived. *(In the earlier version of the story Bill wrote 'Grapevine' in brackets above Blue Ball and added a question mark. He was right, it was Grapevine.)*

As John Perryman turned the corner to walk down the side of the bank, someone on top and at the other end, blasted at him with a shotgun. The charge struck him in the chest, and although he managed to reach home by way of the hillside path, he died soon afterwards.

A short distance down the road from 'Blue Ball' and towards the church is 'Grapevine', and here Agnes Ward (my great aunt), then aged nine, and in charge of even younger children, heard someone run past the house but did not look out to see who it was. *(In his earlier account, Bill is more specific: 'She heard somebody run down the road past the house'.)* Of course, this may have been someone hurrying to fetch police and doctor, but, because the cottage sported a clock she had a fair idea of the time, and seemed to think that this was before the alarm was raised.

Later that month Inspector de Schmid arrested three people: William Dowell, his sister Mrs Williams, and a neighbour, Amos French. William Dowell was charged with murder, and the other two with being accessories. Mrs Williams' three children were left to fend for themselves, and she and the two men were lodged in the cells at Honiton. A total lack of evidence ensured that the case got no further than the magistrates court.

William Dowell, after learning his trade as a carpenter, seems to have worked in the Birmingham area, or to have travelled the country chasing the best money. By 1881 when he was aged 29 he had saved £128, and returned home. Not being one to hide his light he became unpopular. He also owned a shotgun.

The theory was that he had shot John Perryman in mistake for David Pile with whom he had had a row about something. Also the three people arrested lived close by the church which is just down the road from 'Grapevine' where Agnes Ward heard someone run past. This may have something to do with his arrest.

No red carpet awaited their return, and a very bad 'atmosphere' prevailed for a very long time. The ceremony of burning in effigy was performed on the cliff top across from the church and a cobbler, and close neighbour of Mrs Williams, who was in the habit of giving the children sweets was given the same treatment. *(There is more detail in the earlier version: 'the cobbler/shoe-maker was greatly distressed to hear the shout: "Burn the snob" from the cliff top. "It went through me like a knife," he said.')* This preyed on his mind so that eventually he hanged himself, or so my great aunt said.

Mrs Williams' husband was an inmate of Exminster Mental Hospital with no hope of release, and it came to be thought that the action had been between David Pile and Amos French because both wished to become overfriendly with her. David Pile was supposed to have been overheard to say that he had shot the wrong man, but to whom he said it, or who overheard him say it, was not known. Possibly this was a facetious remark which he found amusing at the time, but less so afterwards. He seems not to have owned a gun or to have access to one unless, of course, he was closely related to John Pile who was the farmer for whom John Perryman was working at the time.

My great aunt also mentioned a well dressed young man armed with a shotgun who was seen around and about the area, and who was thought to be a holiday maker. However, no-one knew who he was or where he came from and he was not seen after the shooting. At the time I had forgotten that my aunt had told me about this man when I was very young. She told me that my grandfather (then aged 26) had seen him twice; once walking along Higher Lane, [3] and once on the road leading towards Sellers Wood. Also a friend of his, whose name I have forgotten, met, spoke to him, but was ignored when they passed each other on Vicarage Hill.

However the arrest of the three people effectively distracted attention from him.

My aunt also told me that a gun was found in a barn somewhere. My wife Eileen said that one was found in a linhay on the cliffs.

My great aunt told me that my grandfather [4] had, presumably with others, gone to the scene of the shooting to gather up John Perryman's belongings. He found the experience frightening in the extreme because of the bright moonlight and the thought that the gunman could still be lurking nearby. Probably he had it in mind that this was the work of what would then have been described as a criminal lunatic. *(Talking to us, Bill mentioned the possibility of 'full-moon madness'.)*

I suspect that this man came in from the direction of Beer. That he walked the roads, lanes and footpaths only, spoke to no-one, and probably shot nothing. If he behaved in this manner he could remain anonymous to all except the police who must have known about him. Also the local press knew of his existence.[5]

* * *

The details Bill gives of Agnes Ward's recollections are very important. She is the only person who mentions:

- the very bad atmosphere in the village after the hearing.
- the burning in effigy on the cliff top across from the church of Bill Dowell, Eliza Williams and Amos French.
- The burning in effigy of a cobbler, a close neighbour of Mrs Williams, who had given sweets to her children, and who hanged himself.

- The anxiety that her brother felt when, on the night of a full moon, he went to the site of the shooting; the fear that a madman might be lurking there; and the possibility that the shooting might have been done by an outsider.

The whole of our Chapter 17 owes a lot to Agnes Ward's telling of the story, and Bill's remembering. Not surprisingly, there are some discrepancies between Bill's account and our findings, and we mention them in case the reader is confused:

- Newspaper accounts make it clear that the man with the gun was down-slope from Perryman rather than on the bank above him.
- Bill's description of the site of the shooting is not the same as ours. It seems to conflate the place where Loveridge and Perryman parted company with the place lower down the hill where Perryman, having walked through Old Pits, was shot. If he had not been killed he would indeed have 'turned a corner to walk down the side of a bank'.
- Perryman did not reach his house alive.
- We believe Dowell when he says that he did not own a shotgun, but had occasionally used one belonging to his brother-in-law.
- We found no evidence for the presence of an armed outsider, and the cutting kept by Bill Carpenter actually refers to Bill Dowell and is mentioned in his pamphlet.

NOTES

Abbreviations

BPOH	Branscombe Project Oral History
DEDG	*Devon & Exeter Daily Gazette*
Dowell	W. D. Dowell: *The Branscombe Murder. The Life of William Dean Dowell, the Accused Murderer*
D.R.O.	Devon Record Office
DWT	*Devon Weekly Times*
EXP	*Exeter Flying Post*
LSJ	*Lethaby's Sidmouth Journal*
PWN	*Pulman's Weekly News*
TDA	*Transactions of the Devonshire Association*
TLS	*Times Literary Supplement.*

Preface

[1] D.H. Lawrence: *Memoir of Maurice Magnus.* D.R. Godine, London, 1987. The quotation is from Lawrence's introduction, cited in a letter by J.Worthen, *TLS,* 24.7.2009.
[2] Footstepping, as the word suggests, is about walking, literally and consciously, in the path of another person's life. Of course it is impossible to take on someone else's experiences, but one can approach closer to them by following in their tracks. The approach was pioneered in Richard Holmes: *Footsteps: Adventures of a Romantic Biographer.* Hodder & Stoughton Ltd, London, 1985.
[3] We are grateful to Phil Planel for discussion on this point, and for directing us towards an article by Robert Macfarlane in the *Guardian* (30.7.2005) in which he cites Kavanagh.
[4] Mary Beard reviewing T. P. Wiseman*: Remembering the Roman People. TLS,* 15.5.2009.
[5] Since then we have found another copy of the pamphlet, in pristine condition, in Sidmouth Museum.

Introduction

[1] *LSJ,* 1.11.1871.
[2] W. H. Hudson: 'Branscombe and its Birds'. *Longmans Magazine,* CXCII, 1898.

[3] The coal-yard is now the courtyard behind the Sea Shanty beach café.
[4] *The Observer*, 7.9.1887.
[5] Culverwell and Culverhole are interchangeable names for both the hill and the farm situated on it. We have used the first form throughout.
[6] A truck-shop is similar to a company shop. People receive part of their wages in vouchers which can only be redeemed at the shop.
[7] One of the Tucker girls was blind for several years, and three had poor eyesight, probably from working on lace patterns by inadequate candle-light. Only Mary, who designed lace, was allowed two candles a night. Barbara Farquharson & Joan Doern: *The Branscombe Lace-Makers*. Branscombe Project 2002. See also M. Tomlinson: *Three Generations in the Honiton Lace Trade*. Sovereign Printing Group, Sidmouth, 1983, pp. 59-60.
[8] Dowell, p. 25.
[9] Dowell, p. 27.
[10] *DWT*, 3.11.1871.
[11] W. H. Hudson: 'Branscombe and its Birds'. *Longmans Magazine*, CXCII, 1898.
[12] It's interesting to compare the sizes of neighbouring settlements. In the 1883 Kelly's Directory the village of Sidbury has around 1,300 inhabitants, and the towns of Honiton and Sidmouth 3,350 and 3,500 respectively.
[13] Talking about a somewhat later period when the water pipes were laid through the village, Lily Gush said: 'They brought the water down through the village and down the hill somewhere. And dad was paying rent. They digged up our garden, and they wouldn't bring we a tap! Couldn't spend no money – that's how they'd got so much!' BPOH transcript.
[14] Shutes are springs piped to an outlet for public use. There are at least six in Branscombe, at Vicarage, Bank, Bridge, near the Church, and two at Street.
[15] B. Farquharson & J. Doern: *Branscombe Shops, Trades & Getting By*. Branscombe Project, 2000.
[16] *Wynne Clarke*: 'An old person, like Mrs Somers mother, Cora Dowell, she used to lay people out. And if anybody gave birth, you could always rely on them to come. They weren't nurses, they were just doing a job. Gifted, you might say.' B. Farquharson & J. Doern: *Branscombe Shops, Trades and Getting By*. Branscombe Project, 2000.
[17] W. H. Hudson: 'Branscombe and its Birds'. *Longmans Magazine,* CXCII, 1898.
[18] So, for example, Bill Dowell visiting his neighbour Amos French: 'Amos French came to the house, and said, "Well, old man, how be 'ee getting on?" I replied, "I believe that pig's tail is the end 'o pork."' *PWN*, 9 October 1883.
[19] BPOH transcript.
[20] Dowell, p. 22.
[21] E. Chick: 'Branscombe Memories'. *The Methodist Recorder*, Winter 1903.

[22] H. S. Daniels: 'The Branscombe Smugglers!' *Western Morning News*, undated cutting.
[23] Dowell, p. 22.
[24] In November 1867, in Sidmouth, the properties of Mr Webber, Mr Pidsley, Mr W. Russell, and Mr Hunt were all damaged, *LSJ*, 1.12.1867. The following year a considerable display of force was on parade in Sidmouth and November 5th passed off without incident.

Chapter 1

[1] Clock time throughout the book is that used in September 1883, i.e. GMT. (British Summer Time was not introduced until 1916.) To imagine the September scene by our clock, the reader must add one hour.
[2] The pits were not entirely disused. Flint waste was still knapped for buildings, and used for road repairs.
[3] The pits in the field have gone now – Angela Gibbons of Pitt farm remembers that in the 1970s her husband Bob filled them with old machinery and levelled them off. See also Appendix D.

Chapter 2

[1] *LSJ* 10.1883.
[2] According to George Chaloner, there were two chapels in the 1860s, one at each end of the village, but by 1871 the lower chapel had become a Free Church (*LSJ*, 1.11.1871). This is the only mention we know of a lower chapel and it seems to have gone out of use by 1881. It might have stood next to (New) Castle cottage.
[3] Elijah Chick was a grandson of Samuel Chick of Berry Barton. This account of the chapel is taken from his 'Branscombe Memories' in *The Methodist Recorder*, Winter 1903. He also tells another story of early chapel days: 'The parson (*sic*) was on one occasion disturbed by the twanging of the bass viol strings and the sundry creakings of the pegs during the sermon. In despair he exclaimed, "Put away that thing." From the gallery came the honest truth in answer, "He's down, Zur, an a'most be drad op."'
[4] The arm-twister would certainly have been John Perryman, and we can take this story further. Chaloner recalls that a few years previously, in the mid-1860s, 'when very weak I laid in a store of health, during a fortnight's pleasant rest [at Branscombe] secured for me by one of the kindest men I ever knew'. He mentions no names, only says that on one occasion, he 'secured a bat, that had had the temerity to fly into our kitchen, driving an old lady into a corner, and two damsels into a capacious cupboard, out of harm's way' The 1861 census lists John

Perryman living at Blue Ball with his wife Sarah, aged 50, and two daughters aged 16 and 19. It seems likely that Chaloner was lodging with them.
[5] Dowell, p. 33.
[6] *LSJ*, 1.10.1883. William Tidwell later became a Methodist preacher, and William Williams was employed by George Butter, the village baker, a peripatetic Wesleyan preacher who thought nothing of walking to Ottery (8 miles) or Fenny Bridges (12 miles) and back on a Sunday. Agnes Ward: *Early History of Methodism in Branscombe*. MS, 1954, p. 3.
[7] D.R.O. 239A add 3 PO 28.
[8] Another of the Grapevine cottages was occupied for a while by John Perryman's sister Jane, with her husband Edmund Upright. He was from Exeter and described himself in the census as a lace manufacturer, while Jane kept a shop, so they were probably dealing in lace made in the village. They may have fallen foul of John Tucker at Barnells, who claimed a monopoly of village lace-making, for they soon moved to Colyton.
[9] J. Y. A. Morshead, *Branscombe Smuggling Stories*, MS, 21.4.1893.
[10] After her husband's death Sarah Perryman moved to Poole, where George Clark was then living on a naval pension, and stayed with him and Mary Ann until she died in 1889.

Chapter 3

[1] John Pile was David Pile's second cousin, a widower of 67 who lived at Street with an unmarried daughter. Samuel Wyatt, 42, was the brother of David Pile's next-door neighbour William Wyatt.
[2] *PWN*, 2.10.1883.
[3] The young man who helped Tidwell and Williams carry Perryman down the hill was Thomas Ward, the son of Perryman's next-door neighbour at Grapevine, so Ephraim Perryman must have run out from the end house to help bring in the corpse.
[4] *PWN*, 9.10.1883.
[5] Dowell, p. 10.
[6] William Ward was the elder brother of Thomas Ward, and Mark Newton was younger brother of Thomas Newton, one of the Edge Farm harvesters.
[7] William Ward told this story to Bill Carpenter. See Appendix D.
[8] *PWN*, 18.9.1883.
[9] Amos Power took over the lease of Elverway farm in 1882, but he kept the lease of Culverwell farm and let it to a dairyman, George Bright.
[10] The house no longer exists.
[11] 'Moor' here probably means a marshy place. A gamekeeper first appears in the Branscombe census in 1871, soon after Henry Ford had bought the manor from the

Ecclesiastical Commissioners. The previous landowners, the Dean and Chapter of Exeter, presumably let shooting rights to the tenant farmers. Fred Skinner was a recent appointment, born in Ottery St Mary and aged 28 in 1883.
[12] Woodhouse Farm and Wobble Cottage would have been on their way.

Chapter 4

[1] *EFP,* 26.9.1883.
[2] *PWN*, 25.9.1883.
[3] *EFP*, 12.9.1883.
[4] *PWN*, 18.9.1883.
[5] *LSJ,* 1.10.1883.

Chapter 5

[1] There were probably eight jurors. Of the four who spoke during the inquest and were named in the press, John Ellis, William Pike and Robert Salter were farmers, the last two being tenants of Henry Ford, while the fourth, John Collins, was an elderly 'boot-makers kit-maker', Cornish by origin, a tenant of Samuel Chick at Street, and like him a Methodist.
[2] No relation of Thomas and John Pile, the harvesters at Edge Farm mentioned in Chapter 3. The spelling of all these surnames varied between Pile and Pyle.
[3] Robert Loveridge died in 1920, aged 80.
[4] *PWN,* 18.9.1883; 2.10.1883.
[5] D.R.O. 1037M/ E 2/3.
[6] Thomas Newton died in 1915 at the age of 60, having fathered eight children.
[7] There were four cottages at Blue Ball, the property of John Gill.
[8] William Bartlett was a naval serviceman when he married in 1853. He and his wife both died in 1913, aged 83.
[9] The bakery is now the Old Bakery tearooms.
[10] *PWN*, 18.9.1883. Here, as throughout, spoken words are quoted from the newspaper accounts in *Pulman's Weekly* or *the Exeter Flying Post*. Not all the questions put to witnesses were reported and we have constructed some to fit the answers that follow them. We have also replaced formal newspaper terms such as 'the deceased', 'the witness', etc. with the persons' names, also replaced third-person with first-person pronouns where appropriate, and occasionally modernised punctuation.

Chapter 6

[1] Even then, in the case of the murder at Road in 1860 it was not until the local police investigation had been ridiculed in the national press that the Wiltshire magistrates asked the Home Office to send a detective from the Met. Kate Summerscale: *The Suspicions of Mr Whicher*. London, Bloomsbury, 2008.
[2] Dowell, p.13.
[3] De Schmid's first taste of police work was quelling a riot in Honiton in December 1882 by the Skeleton Army, a thuggish organization created by Devon brewers and publicans to drive out and defeat the Salvation Army's new gospel of teetotalism. Arrests were made but there were no convictions. Magistrates were unsympathetic to the Salvation Army, perhaps because it threatened the (cheap) tradition of paying farm workers' overtime in cider. D.R.O. Devon Quarter Sessions Box, Epiphany 1883: Chief Constable's Report, January 1883; J. Robin: *The Way We Lived Then*. Ashgate Publishing, Aldershot, 2000, pp. 148-9.
[4] N. J. P. Aggett, *The Bloody Eleventh, History of the Devonshire Regiment*, vol.2.
[5] Obituary in *TDA*, vol. 21, p. 71.
[6] John Perryman's name was spelt Perriman in newspapers and in Dowell's pamphlet, but we have used the form that is on his gravestone and in parish registers.
[7] Dowell, pp. 14-16. The pub can bc identified as The Masons Arms by the name of the landlady, Mrs Clarke.
[8] Dowell, p.16.
[9] Dowell, p. 18.
[10] *PWN*, 25.9.1883.
[11] Dowell, p. 19.
[12] Dowell, p. 16.
[13] Dowell, p. 20.
[14] This almost equalled an agricultural worker's annual wage.

Chapter 7

[1] On the use of oxen for ploughing, Lilian Pike of Branscombe recalled that her father Richard Pike was apprenticed to the blacksmith at Bridge, and that one year he spent 'the whole of one winter's night shoeing oxen up at Hedge Barton [Edge] … ready for work on the frozen ground'. Kingsley Squire: 'Shotgun blast that blew a village apart', *Express and Echo,* 31.3.1955.
[2] Dowell, p. 5. Possibly these Tuckers were relatives of his grandmother Sarah Tucker. Village gossip (from a later period) claimed that Bill Dowell's father, John Tucker Dowell, after selling Branscombe cheeses in Sidmouth, would drink the proceeds, be put insensible into his cart, and be taken home by his horse.

[3] Dowell, p. 25.
[4] This account of the Ford-Tomkins dispute is based on correspondence in D.R.O. 1037M/ LG8/1.
[5] Dowell, p. 26.
[6] Dowell, p. 26.
[7] Dowell, p. 5.
[8] Dowell, p. 6.
[9] Dowell, p. 22.
[10] Dowell, p. 6.
[11] *EFP*, 26.9.1883.
[12] Dowell, p. 7.
[13] Dowell, pp. 17; 24. They were charged with indecent assault on Emma Jane Lockyer and sentenced to three months hard labour in January 1883.
[14] Dowell, p.18.
[15] *PWN*, 9.10.1883; Dowell, p. 8.
[16] *PWN*, 2.10.1883.
[17] Dowell, pp. 27;14.
[18] *Pulman's* acknowledged his contribution (18.9.1883) but used its own report.
[19] *PWN*, 2.10.1883.
[20] *PWN*, 9.10.1883, 25.9.1883.
[21] *EFP*, 3.10.1883, *PWN*, 2.10.1883.
[22] Dowell, pp. 16-17.
[23] Dowell, p. 24.
[24] Dowell, pp. 20-21.
[25] Dowell, pp. 20, 9.
[26] Dowell, pp. 22-23.
[27] Dowell, p. 22.
[28] Dowell, p. 21.
[29] Dowell, p. 27.

Chapter 8

[1] The Rev. Thomas Puddicombe, registering the burial of three sailors drowned when the Danish-crewed ship *Omen* was wrecked at Branscombe in 1802, added that 'She had on board twelve Hands besides the Captain and a boy. Ten of the Hands and the Boy were saved'. If Matthew Westbye was the boy, he was six or less at the time! In 1820 his marriage, under the name Matthew Westbye alias Williams, was witnessed by William Westbye alias Williams, which suggests that at that date he had a father or brother in England, who like him had adopted an English name.

[2] J. Y. A. Morshead: *Branscombe Smuggling Stories*, MS, April 21, 1893. Morshead gave the name of his informant as William Gill, 71, but there was no such person in Branscombe. Probably he mistook the name, and we have assumed that his informant was John Gill, b. 1822, whose brother William had died in 1865.
[3] Jack Rattenbury (1778-1844) was a celebrated Beer smuggler who wrote *Memoirs of a Smuggler* in 1837. Matthew Williams's supplies, if arranged in England, may have come through William Mutter, a member of a notorious smuggling family. Mutter passed himself off as an Exmouth fisherman, but the Customs service believed he was the Agent of a Company and regarded him as the principal smuggler on this coast. He was jailed for six months at Penzance in 1851, and again at Exeter in 1857. National Archives, CUST 33/131.
[4] F. Graham: *Smuggling in Devon*. Lyme Regis, 1986, p. 24. On Samual Bray, see R. F. Chapple: *Old Smuggling Days in East Devon*. Axe Valley Heritage Association, 2003, pp. 27-8.
[5] A list of rules for the choir promulgated in 1850 was signed by the members, including, besides the three Williams and Matthew Williams's smuggling partner John Gill, the three Dowell thatchers mentioned in Chapter 7. Matthew Williams junior was said to have 'read the Bible from cover to cover and to be able to quote reams of it'. H. S. Daniel: 'The Branscombe Smugglers!' *Western Morning News*, undated cutting.
[6] H. S. Daniel, as above. John Williams gave up The Masons Arms before 1881, but remained a butcher, living at Wootons on Vicarage Hill. His eldest daughter Ellen married (1879) Edwin Leonard, a naval serviceman, and the butcher's business eventually passed to her son, Burgess Edwin Leonard. See Farquharson & Doern: *Shops, Trades and Getting By*. Branscombe Project, 2000.
[7] Henry Ford bought John Williams's cottages when he died. D.R.O. 1037M/LG 8/11.
[8] R. Grimley: *Up Over and Down Through*. Kingsbridge, 2009, p. 36. In 1884 William Williams rented 46 acres at Cliff. D.R.O. 1037M/ LG 8/12.
[9] The death certificate reads 'whilst temporarily insane', the customary words used to avoid the harsh legal consequences of suicide, which was still a crime. But given the family's mental record, it may be true.
[10] All this from H. S. Daniel: 'The Branscombe Smugglers!' *Western Morning News*, undated cutting.
[11] D.R.O. 3769A/ H2/ 31, 43; 3769A/ H3/8; 1037M/ E7/4.
[12] D.R.O. 3767A/H2/35b. The certificate was signed by the Rev. R. Swansborough and John Trick, Relieving Officer, Honiton Poor Law Union.
[13] *PWN*, 9.10.1883.
[14] In the 1883 Berry farm rent book there were 34 plat-holders, of which only three paid less rent than Eliza.
[15] D.R.O. 239A add 3 PO 28.

[16] *EFP*, 26.9.1883.
[17] *PWN*, 16.10.1883.
[18] *PWN*, 25.9.1883.
[19] *PWN*, 2.10.1883.
[20] *PWN*, 16.10.1883.

Chapter 9

[1] This comes from *Pulman's* account; the *Exeter Flying Post* said there were mainly farmers and others. The 'others', no doubt, were the women!
[2] *EFP*, 26.9.1883.
[3] Dowell, p. 8.
[4] *PWN*, 9.10.1883.
[5] Dowell, p. 8.
[6] *PWN*, 2.10.1883. Quoted speech in this chapter comes from this edition of *Pulman's* unless otherwise noted.
[7] Dowell, p. 12.
[8] *PWN*, 9.10.1883.
[9] *EFP*, 26.9.1883.
[10] *PWN*, 9.10.1883.
[11] A drangway is a narrow lane or passage.
[12] Dowell, pp. 7-8.
[13] *PWN*, 9.10.1883.
[14] *PWN*, 9.10.1883.
[15] Dowell, p. 8.

Chapter 10

[1] *PWN*, 2.10.1883. Quoted speech in this chapter comes from this edition of *Pulman's* unless otherwise noted.
[2] *EFP*, 26.9.1883.
[3] Dowell, p. 19.
[4] Dowell, p. 11. Another 'deliberate lie' with which Dowell charged Martin concerned their visit to Skinner's house. Martin stated to the inquest that 'He had some conversation with Skinner, and just as they were leaving, Dowell said "Have you got a drop of brandy in the house? I feel awful queer. I should like a drop."' In his pamphlet, Dowell replied 'The scoundrel, I would not have asked for anything had it not been for him'. And he explained: 'On the road Martin says to me, "I feel rather thirsty. I could drink a drop of cider." I said, "So could I, and when I get over to Skinner's I will ask him if he has any in the house. ... and as we were leaving I said to Skinner, "Have you a drop of cider in the house you could give

us?" He said "No, I wish I had, Bill!" and then I said, in a jocular manner, "Have you a drop of brandy," and he said, "No!"'

[5] Dowell, pp. 11-12.

[6] Dowell, p. 16.

[7] There was no George Williams. Dowell probably said 'Thomas Williams', referring to Eliza's insane husband. This store of powder and shot indicates that Collier's old gun was a muzzle-loader. Cartridges were a recent innovation.

[8] *PWN*, 9.10.1883.

Chapter 11

[1] *PWN*, 2.10.1883. Reportage and quoted speech in this chapter comes from this edition of *Pulman's* unless otherwise noted.

[2] 'Most of the men wore suits of stiff, dark brown corduroy, or, in the summer, corduroy trousers and an unbleached drill jacket known as a "sloppy"'. F. Thompson: *Lark Rise to Candleford.* London, Oxford University Press, 1963, p. 38. It sounds as if Perryman and Pile were wearing sloppies.

[3] A deed from 1902 in the possession of Sue Brewer of Country House, the present owner of the field, refers to the 'cottages and gardens and premises called Upper Church Cottages bounded by a private road leading to allotment ground belonging to Henry Ford'. Collick's Cottage (Windycott) was probably the former farm house of Collick's Farm.

[4] *EFP*, 3.10.1883.

[5] De Schmid added that 'I examined the gun produced last Sunday, and found an exploded cap upon it. In my opinion the gun had been fired within a month or six weeks'. Parrett's gun would have been a muzzle-loader, fired by means of a cylindrical copper percussion cap placed over a hollow nipple at the end of the barrel. When the hammer struck the primer (a small quantity of shock-sensitive explosive set in the base of the cap) a flame would pass through the nipple and ignite the main charge.

Chapter 12

[1] *PWN*, 2.10.1883.

[2] *PWN*, 16.10.1883.

[3] *PWN*, 9.10.1883. Quoted speech in this chapter comes from this edition of *Pulman's* unless otherwise noted.

[4] Horace Pike remembered how 'They'd fill 'em up with flint stones, of a certain size, see, an' then put the sandstone on top o' that', and Brian Dowell, whose father and grandfather got '5p a day or something like that for the whole lot',

added, 'There weren't steam rollers then, they used to just bang 'em down with hammer'. BOHP transcript.

[5] In the 1881 census, Mary Newton, widow, is recorded as 'Grocer', living with her daughter at Street. Hers was probably the same small shop that Agnes Ward ran in later years.

[6] There were thirty-one agricultural workers in Street, and thirty lace-makers. Amongst the people who have already figured in our story Robert Loveridge with his wife Anna Maria and six children lived at Street; so did William Tidwell with his parents; and John and Amelia Dowell, the parents of Eliza and Bill.

[7] Twilight was called 'dimpsey', and Rita Saunders recounts that 'Sometimes, this time of year, it wouldn't be dark enough to have the light on at six o'clock, yet it wouldn't be enough to see [to make lace] by daylight, "between the lights" they always use to call that'. BOHP transcript.

[8] People still remember when, later on, his wife Sarah ran the shop. Wynne Clarke said: 'She was a little short woman, and used to wear a shawl around her shoulders and a little sort of hat. Black, everything was black. She used to shuffle along, not walk like we do, she was more of a shuffler'; and Rita Saunders: 'She'd cut the bacon with the knife, she'd dig out the sweets out of the bottle with the same knife, and I'm still living to tell the tale'. BOHP transcript.

[9] In 1881 there were 12 adults and 18 children living in the six cottages; now they are four dwellings with two permanent residents.

[10] Frederick Williams was the son of William Williams, Eliza's brother-in-law. His wife seems to have been lodging with the Raffells in what had recently been her father's home, possibly because Frederick was in the process of moving to Salcombe Regis, where he became a farmer.

[11] An obscure joke, but the people gathered in the school-room appreciated it and laughed.

[12] In 1881 Bessie was the living-in maid at Bridge Cottage, now the Old Bakery Tearoom, working for the Methodist baker George Butter, but it seems she had moved to the mill by 1883. Also living at Bridge Cottage in 1881 was Butter's apprentice William James Williams, who had run to the aid of Perryman.

[13] The same well at the lower end of Upper Church, now tarmacked over, where David Pile, half an hour later, heard that Perryman had been shot.

[14] *EFP*, 3.2.1883.

[15] *PWN*, 16.10.1883.

[16] *EFP*, 26.9.1883.

[17] There was no earlier evidence on the time taken by Dowell to read the paper and fry the meat. De Schmid may have been referring to the discrepancy between Eliza's and Mrs Northcott's timekeeping.

[18] For example, according to Loveridge Perryman was not in the habit of coming home at a particular time and had not come home at a particular time during the past few weeks. *PWN*, 2.10.1883.
[19] *PWN,* 16.10.1883. Quoted passages in this section and the next come from this edition of *Pulman's* unless otherwise noted.
[20] A gun-wad, for ramming down on the shot to keep it in place after loading, was normally punched out of cardboard or felt.
[21] The gun was found on Saturday 22 September, a fortnight after the shooting.
[22] 'Blue-vinnied' is a dialect word for verdigris.

Chapter 13

[1] *LSJ,* 1.11.1883.
[2] Dowell, p. 20.
[3] D.R.O. 337B/2. The session is not recorded at all in the rough minute book of Honiton Petty Sessions. D.R.O. 337B/9/6.
[4] Dowell, p. 25.
[5] Dowell, p. 25.
[6] Dowell, pp. 23-24.
[7] That is to say, Fred and Lewis Dowell.

Chapter 14

[1] John Gill (born 1855) was a blacksmith working at the forge at Bridge.
[2] We do not know why Eliza let seventeen months pass before Ellen was baptised.
[3] Dowell. p. 13.
[4] Personal communication by Flossie's great-grand-daughter Jane Harris (Holman).
[5] Dowell, p. 20.
[6] *PWN*, 10.2.1885, p.6.

Chapter 15

[1] A hayrick belonging to Mr G. Pyle of Buckerell was set on fire on 8 August 1884, and a barn belonging to Mr Richards at Axmouth on 1 December (*PWN* 11.12.1884). In January 1885 ricks were burned at Ottery St Mary and Feniton (*PWN*, 27.1.1885). Philcombe Farm at Sidbury was burnt in November 1887 (*LSJ* 1.1.1887).
[2] T. Hibbert, 'The Carpet of History Unrolls', *The Branscombe Chronicle*, July 1978.

[3] There is better evidence of unrest during this earlier agricultural depression. Martha Bartlett wrote to her grand-daughter on January 30 1845: 'We have had a riot concerning the poor rates. They want every poor person to pay and there is six poor men bound over for trial to Asizes and farmer Daw had his linhay sat on fire while he was takeing the poor people goods. It is not known who did it.' On June 3 1845 she writes to her son: 'there is a great disturbance in the parish.' (From letters loaned to the Project by Richard Bartlett.)

[4] However one oral tradition suggests that the torching of Berry Barton had more to do with competition between Samuel Chick and Jackie Lee over a woman than with political or economic outrage! (Conversation with Terence Lee.) This must also have been the occasion when, according to Bill Carpenter, his great-uncle Samuel Ward, seeing Berry Barton ablaze, hurried over and helped rescue the furniture. He burnt one of his boots and when he asked Henry Ford, owner of the farm, for a new pair, he was given *one* boot. No wonder Henry Ford was unpopular!

[5] The Conservative Party's instruction to Conservative parish committees was 'To ascertain, by systematic enquiry throughout the parish the names of all householders or occupiers, with their politics'. This and other lists in Henry Ford's papers are the results of such inquiries.

[6] In Devon the Liberals fought the 1885 election partly on the programme of land reform advanced by the Radical group in the party, and Conservatives used the name 'Radical' as a scare-word to frighten moderate Liberals.

[7] BOHP transcript.

[8] This and the next two quotations are from B. Farquharson & J. Doern, *Branscombe Shops, Trades and Getting By*. Branscombe Project, 2000. Henry Pike farmed Berry Barton by 1891. Brian Dowell said: 'My father and his father [George Dowell] used to do the roads. They used to get about a penny a mile for keeping all the ditches clean and all the roads'. BPOH transcript.

[9] Thus, in August 1883 he objected to the inclusion of G. W. Bartlett: 'I cannot think that he will be useful to the Conservative cause'. (His parents were Methodists, and he lived in Cambridge.) 1037M/ E 7/2.

[10] D.R.O. 1037M/ E7/3.

[11] At about the same time Richard Lethaby presided over a Liberal Association meeting in Sidmouth to discuss the same subject. *PWN*, 23.12.1884.

[12] *LSJ*, 11.1884.

[13] *LSJ*, 12.1884.

[14] D.R.O. 1037M/ E7/3.

[15] Dowell, pp. 4; 22.

[16] *DEDG*, 26.6.1885.

Chapter 16

[1] For example in Torquay, 'the Guy Fawkes Day custom of burning before the house or cottage of any unpopular person an effigy carefully dressed to resemble him or her' . M. E. Fielden, 'Living Memories in Devon', *TDA*, vol. 67, 1935, p. 387.
[2] J. Robin: *The Way We Lived Then.* Ashgate Publishing, Aldershot, 2000, p.24.
[3] *DWT,* 10.11.1871, pp. 6, 7; 1/12/1871, p. 7.
[4] The strongest ground for dating it to 1884 rather than 1883 emerges in Chapter 17.
[5] F.Thompson: *Lark Rise to Candleford.* Oxford University Press, London, 1963, p.146. Only one house was visited because the woman's lover was her lodger.
[6] Skimmington processions could take place at any time of year and did not necessarily lead to effigy-burning. In Hardy's *The Mayor of Casterbridge*, the lurid skimmington ride plotted in a pub led to the death of Lucetta Henchard, and was followed by the grisly reappearance of the effigy in the river.
[7] On October 31 1883 P. C. Martin charged two of Thomas Gill's younger brothers, William John (aged 19) and William Charles (aged 16) with being drunk in licensed premises (presumably The Fountain Head) and they were fined. The date of the offence is unclear, but the inquest verdict of wilful murder had been handed down a fortnight earlier, and this drinking-bout may have been one reaction to it, on the part of young men who had probably shared many drinks with Dowell. D.R.O. 337B/9/6.
[8] D.R.O. 1037M/SS1/5.
[9] Dowell, p. 26.
[10] He was fined 2s 6d with 10s costs. *PWN,* 20.1.1885, p. 8.
[11] *PWN,* 7.3.1884.
[12] D.R.O. 239A add 3 PO 28.
[13] D.R.O. 1037M/E2/3. They were probably bought by Ephraim Perryman. Directories of the 1890s list him as the village carrier, with a regular Saturday service to Honiton market.

Chapter 17

[1] Dowell, p. 17.
[2] *LSJ*, 11.1883.
[3] *DWT*, 3.11.1871.
[4] Meanwhile, William and Sarah Bartlett moved down from Blue Ball to Collick's Cottage.
[5] The relative named on her reception order was George Butter, her nephew, who had given up the bakery and become Branscombe's first postmaster. Probably this

devout Methodist had kept an eye on her during the last ten years, although the document gives her religion as 'C of E'.

Chapter 18

[1] We have found no record or report of the inquest on Sam Parrett, which must have been held in Branscombe and was conducted by the same Coroner who conducted the inquest on John Perryman. If he made a connection between the two deaths, it seems not to have affected village opinion.
[2] BPOH transcript.
[3] BPOH transcript.
[4] Dowell, p. 15. His brothers had probably moved from 7 Hindsley Place by this time. No 6 Hindsley Place has since been demolished.
[5] See Appendix D.
[6] *LSJ*, 5.4.1885.
[7] However, it was no longer there in 1925.
[8] His brother Lewis moved to Tunbridge Wells and in the Second World War his wife Jessica came back to Branscombe and lived with Laura Dowell. Her little daughter Elizabeth went to the village school.
[9] The copy of Bill's letter was given us by Flossie's great-grand-daughter, Jane Harris (Holman).
[10] Shown to us by Richard Fisher.
[11] The family was from Braunton in N. Devon.
[12] Agnes Ward, 'Early History of Methodism in Branscombe', MS 1954. Roland French later became a Baptist minister at Ipswich and elsewhere.
[13] A keyboard instrument with bellows worked by foot-pedals, perhaps best known from Patrick Kavanagh's poem 'A Christmas Childhood' — 'My father played the melodeon / Outside at our gate'.

Appendix A

[1] Farms owned by Henry Ford are taken from the Poor Rate book for 1884, but almost certainly had not changed hands since 1881. D.R.O. 1037M// LG8/12.
[2] In the north where farmers had to compete with the new industries for labour, and where there was no payment in kind, wages could be almost double those in the south-west. The Rev. Canon Girdlestone, vicar of Halberton in Devon, who arranged for local farm workers to relocate in order to make labour scarcer, was much abused by farmers and land-owners.

Appendix B

[1] In a later account he said 'five or seven minutes'. *PWN,* 2.10.1883.
[2] *PWN,* 2.10.1883.
[3] *LSJ*, 1.10.1883; *PWN*, 18.9.1883.
[4] *PWN*, 2.10.1883.
[5] That he was lying down is consistent not only with Martin's description of the 'impression' but also with the report that 'the grass had been blackened by the discharge of a gun'. *EFP*, 26.9.1883.
[6] P. C. Martin said that place where man had been lying was about 19 yards from the first spots of blood on the ground (*PWN,* 2.10.1883); Supt. de Schmid said the distance between where the body was found and the impression was scarcely four feet (*PWN* 2.10.1883). This would mean that Perryman staggered more than 50 feet before he fell.
[7] *PWN,* 18.8.1883.
[8] *EFP,* 26.9.1883.
[9] *PWN.* 2.10.1883.

Appendix C

[1] E. Chick, 'Branscombe Memories' *The Methodist Recorder,* Winter 1903, and Agnes Ward's unpublished 'Early History of Methodism in Branscombe', MS 1954.
[2] R. E. Wilson, 'History of Methodism at Branscombe', *Sidmouth Herald,* 9.11.1973. He also mentions Samuel Coombs as an 'early stalwart'.
[3] Ephraim Perryman, a Methodist, was unregistered on the electoral roll, but two of his sons, William and Sydney, appear there as D's. Although probably Methodists, their children were baptised in church, so they are not included here.

Appendix D

[1] B. Farquharson & J. Doern: *Shops, Trades and Getting By*, The Branscombe Project, 2000.
[2] This is a grumble against Government subsidies offered to farmers in the mid-seventies.
[3] Higher Lane is the short lane linking Vicarage Hill to Beach Road.
[4] Bill's grand-father was William Ward. He was the brother of Agnes Ward and was twenty-six at the time of the shooting.
[5] A small cutting, which Bill Carpenter had kept, says: 'It is rumoured that the shot was intended for someone else, and that a certain individual had left the

neighbourhood since the occurrence. Three arrests were made, but the police were unable to prove anything definite against the persons, and they were discharged.'